HISTORY O

A BRIEF TEXT BOOK FOR SCHOOLS

BY

ROYALL BASCOM SMITHEY, A.M., Litt.D.

AUTHOR OF CIVIL GOVERNMENT OF VIRGINIA

REVISED EDITION

AMERICAN BOOK COMPANY

NEW YORK   CINCINNATI   CHICAGO

To My Wife

ANNIE SHACKELFORD SMITHEY

I DEDICATE THIS BOOK

G. Washington

PREFACE

————◆◆◆————

IN this volume, I have endeavored to present in a clear
and connected manner the leading facts in the history of
Virginia. The materials have been drawn from the most
reliable authorities, and much time has been spent in com-
paring them so as to render the narrative as accurate as
possible. In the colonial period, the richness of the
sources of information proved a continual embarrassment;
and I found myself compelled to leave out many interesting incidents, to prevent the book from exceeding the
well-defined limits within which a state history for school
use should be kept.

Virginia was the cradle of the English race in America,
and for this reason her history is of more than ordinary
interest. Besides this, the great variety of romantic and
important events that have taken place within her borders, the immortal characters that have been nurtured
upon her soil, and the unswerving manner in which her
people have always contended for their rights, render her
history specially worthy of being studied. Of all the emo-
tions that stir the human soul, love of country is one of

the noblest; and near akin to it is reverence for one's ancestors. If this little book shall have the happy effect of increasing the patriotism of young people, and of causing them to appreciate more highly the deeds of their forefathers, the author will feel amply repaid for his labor.

R. B. SMITHEY.

RANDOLPH-MACON COLLEGE, VA.

CONTENTS

—◦◦—

INTRODUCTION

FIRST PERIOD — THE COLONY

CHAPTER I

CHAPTER II

CHAPTER III

CHAPTER XI

CHAPTER XII

CHAPTER XIII

CHAPTER XIV

SECOND PERIOD—FROM THE REVOLUTION TO THE CIVIL WAR

CHAPTER XV

CHAPTER XXXI

HISTORY OF VIRGINIA

—•o°o°o•—

INTRODUCTION

THE FIRST INHABITANTS

The Indians of Virginia. — When the territory now included in Virginia was first settled by the English, it was occupied by an Indian population numbering about ten thousand, divided among more than forty clans or tribes. Each of these was ruled over by a chief; and about thirty of them were united in a loose confederacy under a head-chief named Powhatan. There were also two smaller confederacies and a few scattering tribes which maintained their independence. All the Virginia Indians belonged to the great Algonkin [1] family.

Appearance. — The Virginia Indians were manly in appearance, being tall, straight, and well-proportioned. They were copper-colored, had high cheek bones, piercing black

---

[1] The Algonkin Indians occupied the eastern coast of North America from the St. Lawrence River to North Carolina, and in the interior nearly all the territory that was south of the Great Lakes and east of the Mississippi. All the Algonkin Indians had similar customs and spoke cognate languages. The origin of the Indians is unknown. They possessed no written history, and their traditions as to their ancestors were conflicting. The theory that at a very remote age they reached America from Asia by way of Bering Strait has many advocates, and is possibly true. America, when first discovered, was supposed to be a part of India, and for this reason the aboriginal inhabitants were called "Indians" by the early explorers.

eyes, and coarse black hair. The women wore their hair long and allowed it to hang over their shoulders. The men cut theirs short on one side, but let it grow long on the other. On the top of their heads, they carefully preserved a lock or ridge, like a cock's comb, which was called the scalp lock. This was the warrior's pride and

Virginia Indian

his token of defiance to his enemies, whom he dared to take it. Their clothing was made chiefly of the skins of the deer, the raccoon, the beaver, and the otter. Their shoes were made of buckskin, and were called moccasins. They possessed in a high degree the fondness for ornaments and toys that has been observed in all savages. They tattooed their bodies with representations of flowers, fruits, and birds, and adorned themselves with handsome mantles made of curiously interwoven feathers, which were dyed red or blue, as fancy dictated. Their heads and shoulders they painted red, with the juice of the blood-root plant; and both men and women wore necklaces of beads and pearls. Altogether, they were a curious and picturesque looking race.

Their Character. — Bravery and fortitude were good qualities which the Indians generally possessed. But they were cruel, vindictive, and treacherous. They had no laws to restrain evil doers; and so, when a man was wronged by another, he had to punish the offender himself. In this way, the spirit of revenge was so cultivated that it became an Indian's pride never to forget an injury. He would carefully conceal his resentment, while he waited long years for an opportunity to wreak his vengeance; and when it came, he would execute the penalty with interest. Thus it happened that among them it was the custom to return evil for evil. Their training gave them no idea of the golden rule; and so they knew not how to render good for evil, though at times they would repay kindness with kindness.

Weapons. — Bows and arrows, stone hatchets, called tomahawks, stone knives, wooden spears and clubs con-

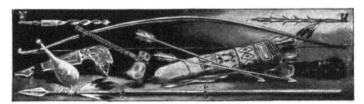

Indian Weapons

stituted their chief weapons. In hunting, they depended mainly upon the bow and arrow, which by constant practice they learned to use with great skill. They could discharge their arrows with so much force that they were able to bring down their game at a distance of more than a hundred yards. The arrows were winged with turkey feathers and had heads made of stone. Specimens of these arrowheads are still found in Virginia.

Wigwams. — The Indians dwelt in villages, chiefly along the banks of the numerous rivers that flow through Virginia. They constructed their cabins, which were called wigwams, by driving stakes in the ground and fastening

VIRG. HIST. — 2

them together at the top by means of bent poles. They covered them with reeds, bark, and skins. These rude houses were sometimes fifty or a hundred feet long; and some of them exhibited a slight advance toward civiliza-

Wigwams

tion by being divided into separate rooms. At the top, a small opening was left for smoke to escape. If the fire on the hearth went entirely out, this was regarded by the women as an evil omen, and accordingly it was rarely allowed to occur. For chairs the Indians used mats, and for beds they constructed raised platforms, which were covered with mats and skins.

Habits and Customs. — They engaged in agriculture to a limited extent, cultivating corn, beans, and tobacco. As they possessed no iron or steel instruments to fell the forests, where their crops were to be planted, they girdled the trees with stone hatchets, cutting the bark away in a ring, which stopped the flow of the sap and caused the trees to die. This practice, which originated with the savages, is still used in parts of Virginia. All work was performed by women, or squaws, as they were called, the men spending their time in hunting, fishing, and in fighting their enemies. When the Indians went off on long hunting expeditions, the women carried the burdens, and when the day drew to a close cut down saplings and built arbors, while the warriors looked complacently on, smoking their pipes, or else practiced shooting at targets.

Indian Warfare. — The savages were usually in a state of warfare with tribes that were hostile to them. They never fought a pitched battle, nor did they contend in an open field, but depended upon strategy, surprises, and silent approaches. Their method was to entrap their enemies in ambuscades, or else to creep upon them in Indian file, and attack them unexpectedly. Prisoners, especially women

Running the Gantlet

and children, were frequently adopted into the tribe, but many were tortured to death.

Running the Gantlet. — A favorite method of torture, called running the gantlet, was to compel a captive to run between two rows of warriors, each of whom would strike him with a club or knife, as he passed along. At times, a prisoner would escape torture if he showed bravery in a high degree, so much did the savages value this quality.

A marked example of this occurred in the case of General Stark of New Hampshire. The Indians captured him, and decided that he must run the gantlet. Stark saw death staring him in the face; but as he started, he snatched a club from one of the savages, and swinging it right and left, rushed on between the lines of astonished warriors, laying them out as he went along. Thus he passed through the ordeal almost unhurt. The savages loudly applauded his daring, and the old men laughed at the young braves who had been so unceremoniously knocked over. Instead of torturing Stark again, they bestowed upon him the honors of a hero.

Education. — The Indians were quick of apprehension and ingenious. They learned what they could from nature, finding out the habits of animals and discovering the properties of plants. Nothing escaped their notice. So well did they train their ears and eyes, that, in the forests, they could hear sounds and see sights which could not be perceived by a white man; and they could travel with ease for miles in a straight line through the thickest woods. The boys and girls were taught how to make earthen pots, to fashion stone hatchets and arrowheads, and to manufacture beads out of the shells found on the seacoast. Beyond such rude arts as these, their education did not extend. Their idea of numbers was very limited. It is said that some of them could count only ten, while others could reckon a thousand. "As numerous as pigeons in the woods or as the stars in the heavens," was the way they expressed a large number. Some years after the English arrived at Jamestown, Powhatan sent Tomocomo, one of his chiefs, over to England with instructions to find out the population of the country. Tomocomo carried along with him a bundle of sticks, and he was ordered to

cut a notch for every Englishman he met. The story
tells us that he diligently followed his instructions till he
reached London, when, amazed by the multitude he saw
thronging the streets, his arithmetic failed him, and, throwing away his sticks, he gave up the undertaking.

How they Looked upon Self-control. — From infancy,
they were taught to bear pain patiently and silently. The
boys played a game of "Choosing Chief," in which each
one would press a live coal to his naked body in order to
see who could hold it there the longest, and the successful
one was honored by being selected leader. A story told
by an early missionary, also illustrates the value which
the savages placed upon self-control. A great bear was
wounded by an Indian, and groaned piteously as he lay
on the ground. The Indian, hearing this, addressed him
as follows: "Bear, you are a coward and no warrior.
Your tribe and mine are at war, and yours began it. Had
you wounded me, I should not have uttered a sound, while
here you are bringing disgrace upon your tribe."

Seasons and Festivals. — They counted their years by
winters, which they called "Cohonks," from the shrill cry
of the migratory wild geese, which they heard as cold
weather approached. They held a number of feasts, such
as, one for the coming of the wild fowl, one for the return
of the hunting season, and one for the ripening of certain
fruits. But their greatest festival took place at the time
when they gathered corn. This lasted some days and
was frequently participated in by the inhabitants of several
villages. On this occasion, the warriors boasted that, as
their corn had been gathered, which furnished food enough
for the women and children, they were free to hunt, seek
new adventures, or go to war, as they fancied. So they
rejoiced, sang heroic songs, and danced. The historian,

Beverley, describes a festival dance, saying that it is executed by the "dancers themselves forming a ring, and moving around a circle of carved posts, that are set up for that purpose, or else round a fire, made in a convenient part of the town; and then each has his rattle in his hand, or what other thing he fancies most, as his bows and arrows, or his tomahawk. They also dress themselves up with branches of trees, or some other strange accoutrements. Thus they proceed, dancing and singing, with all the antic postures they can invent, and he is the bravest fellow that has the most prodigous gestures."

Religion. — The Indians are represented as believing that when death came they went "beyond the mountains towards the setting sun." One of the earliest writers [1] on Virginia says they believed in "the immortality of the soul, when, life departing from the body, according to the good or bad works it hath done, it is carried up to the tabernacles of the gods to perpetual happiness, or to Popogusso, a great pit, which they think to be at the farthest parts of the world where the sun sets, and there burn continually." They held that it was unnecessary to pray to a good god, for the reason that he would not injure them anyway, but that with the spirit of evil it was different. He might do them harm and so should be appeased. They called him Kiwassa or Okee, and directed their worship to him. They had a legend that once Kiwassa had been on earth; the foundation of the legend is as follows: Below Richmond, about a mile from the James River, there are to be seen on a rock some impressions of unknown origin. They look like the footprints of a giant. To these the Indians pointed, and claimed that they were made by Kiwassa when he came among them.

[1] Thomas Heriot, who went to Virginia with Ralph Lane.

Powhatan. — Powhatan inherited a part of the dominion over which he ruled, and the rest he acquired by conquest. He was among the Indians a kind of rude Napoleon, who had, by conquering tribe after tribe, so increased his ancestral domain that he had risen to some degree of kingly dignity and power. He accomplished this by his bravery, energy, and wisdom. He not only possessed some of the better qualities of human nature, but at times displayed touches of prince-ly magnanimity. From his followers, he exacted many ceremonial observances, and he ruled over them with the authority of a despot. A body-guard of braves attended him by day, and at night sentinels guarded his dwelling while he slept. In 1607, when the history of Virginia really opens, this monarch of the forest was about sixty years old. "His head was somewhat hoary, which, together with his stat-

Powhatan

ure, carriage, and countenance, gave him an air of savage majesty." Naturally he viewed the coming of the English into his domain with alarm; but he was too shrewd and politic to make open war upon them, and so he ended his days in the land of his ancestors. Better would it have been for the Indians of Virginia, had Powhatan's successors followed his example. But instead of doing this, they arrayed themselves against the incoming civilization, and brought on a contest which ended in the destruction of their race.

QUESTIONS

1. How many Indians did the English find in Virginia, and what is said of their clans or tribes?
2. To what great family did they belong?
3. Describe the appearance of the Virginia Indians.
4. Of what did their clothes consist, and how did they show their love of ornament?
5. Give an estimate of the character of the Indian.
6. Why was it their custom to return evil for evil?
7. Describe their weapons.
8. How did they construct their wigwams?
9. Why did they never allow the fire to go out?
10. What did they use for chairs and beds?
11. What products did they cultivate, and how did they clear their lands?
12. What is said of the women or squaws?
13. What was their method of warfare?
14. Explain what was meant by "running the gantlet."
15. What did they learn from nature?
16. What rude arts did they teach their children?
17. Did they have much idea of numbers?
18. On what mission did Powhatan send Tomocomo to London?
19. Give illustrations of how they regarded self-control.
20. How did they count years, and from what was the name derived?
21. Describe their chief festival.
22. Their festival dance.
23. What was the belief of the Indians?
24. Why did they pray to the evil spirit?
25. What legend had they as to their god, Kiwassa?
26. What was Powhatan's position among them?
27. How did he view the coming of the English?

FIRST PERIOD — THE COLONY

CHAPTER I

EARLY ATTEMPTS AT COLONIZATION

Importance of Virginia History. — The history of the English race in America begins with Virginia. Much romantic interest clusters around the first settlement of this famous state, whose soil became the birthplace of a great nation; and a narration of the adventures and deeds of her people constitutes one of the most important parts of the annals of our country.

Why Virginia was Settled. — Toward the close of the sixteenth century, a strong desire to take part in the conquest and settlement of America began to stir the hearts of the English people. To increase trade, to bring heathen peoples under the influence of the Gospel, to have a colony where the surplus of the home population might go, and to check the rising power of Spain were the chief reasons that made England look with longing eyes upon America. Then, too, to found a nation upon the virgin soil of the New World was in itself an attractive thing to the brave, ardent, and restless English people.

Early Explorers. — In 1492, Columbus[1] discovered the

[1] Christopher Columbus, born in Genoa in 1436, or as others say, in 1446, was the son of a wool comber. At the early age of fourteen he evinced such a fondness for the sea that he was allowed to become a sailor. He con-

Bahama Islands, and then later the West Indies and South
America, but he did not reach the continent of North America. In 1497, John Cabot, who commanded an English
fleet, touched upon the mainland, and took possession of
it in the name of England. Upon this fact, England
based her claim to a part of the country; but nearly a
hundred years passed away before she made any effort to
secure it. In 1576, however, Sir Martin Frobisher made
an ineffectual effort to plant a colony; and in 1583, Sir
Humphrey Gilbert made another, in which he lost his life.

Sir Walter Raleigh's Exploring Party. — After the death
of Sir Humphrey Gilbert, his half-brother, Sir Walter
Raleigh,[1] took up the subject of colonization in earnest,

ceived the idea that India could be reached by sailing west from Europe. The
wise men of that day said: "It is absurd. Who is so foolish as to believe that
there are people on the other side of the world, walking with their heels up-
ward and their heads hanging down? And then, how can a ship get there?
The torrid zone, through which it must pass, is a region of fire, where the
very waves boil. And even if a ship could perchance get around there safely,
how could it get back? Can a ship sail uphill?" But Columbus, paying no
attention to such criticisms, persisted for ten years in trying to induce some
European government to send him on a voyage of discovery across the Atlantic, which was then called the "Sea of Darkness." Finally he succeeded in
getting aid from Queen Isabella of Spain, who furnished him with three small
vessels called *Santa Maria*, *Pinta*, and *Niña*. The expedition sailed from
Palos, and after a very eventful voyage, on October 12, 1492, touched on an
island belonging to what is now called the Bahama group. As soon as Columbus landed he fell upon his knees and offered thanks to God. He then took
possession of the land for Spain. On his return to Europe he was received
with great honors by Ferdinand and Isabella. He made a second voyage to
America and founded a colony in Hayti, of which he was appointed governor.
His enemies, from jealousy, maligned him at the court of Spain, so he was
deposed and sent back home in chains. Queen Isabella soon had him released,
but he never recovered from the mortification, and died a sad and disappointed
old man.

[1] Sir Walter Raleigh (1552–1618) was a distinguished soldier and statesman during the reign of Queen Elizabeth. He was also a bold mariner,

and he readily obtained from Queen Elizabeth, who was much interested in the colonization of America, letters patent that gave him all the authority he needed. So he equipped an exploring party, which in April, 1584, he sent

out in two ships under the command of Philip Amidas and Arthur Barlow. This expedition reached the coast of North Carolina in July; and the adventurers landed on an island, called by the Indians Wocokon, near stormy Cape Hatteras. Several days passed, and then some Indians visited them and entertained them in the most hospi-

Raleigh

table manner. The English discovered and explored the island of Roanoke, and after remaining till September, they returned to England and gave a most glowing description of the country.

Origin of the Name Virginia.—The voyagers to the new land said that it was the "most plentiful, sweet, whole-

and on account of his fondness for voyaging, was called the "Shepherd of the Ocean." He won the favor of Queen Elizabeth by his chivalrous attention, and was one of the most attractive and gallant of her courtiers. For seventeen years he was a member of Parliament, and he was one of the commanders of the English fleet that defeated the Spanish Armada. With the death of Elizabeth, the brilliant part of Raleigh's career ended. Finally in 1618, during the reign of James I., he was beheaded on a false charge of treason. He spent forty thousand pounds of his own money on the colonies he sent out. His name is still held in grateful remembrance in Virginia.

some, and fruitful of all other." Marvelous stories were told about the country in the West. There the fruits were more luscious, the flowers more beautiful, the trees taller, the mountains more majestic, than any ever before seen. There, too, the rivers ran over golden beds, and the Fountain of Youth, which removed all traces of age and disease, poured forth its crystal waters. At last, the western paradise foreshadowed by the myths of ancient times had been discovered! Such were the reports of the first explorers, fancy furnishing what facts failed to supply. When Queen Elizabeth, who took pride in being called England's Virgin Queen, heard such charming accounts of the new land, she named it after herself, Virginia.

As to the boundaries of the country, these an old writer described as follows: "The bounds thereof on the East side are the ocean, on the South lieth Florida, on the North Nova Francia [Canada], as for the West thereof the limits are unknown." Since the "South Sea," which was another name for the Pacific Ocean, was supposed to be but a few hundred miles away, this was usually taken as the western boundary. As time passed, the domain called Virginia was continually made smaller, till finally the name was restricted to what is now embraced in the two Virginias.

First Roanoke Island Colony. — Sir Walter Raleigh now made preparations for what he intended to be a permanent settlement. In April, 1585, he sent out a fleet of seven ships under the command of Sir Richard Grenville, which carried to Virginia a colony of 108 persons, Ralph Lane being the governor. These landed on Roanoke Island, and made a settlement. They inquired of the Indians the name of the country, and one of the savages exclaimed, "Wingandacon!" — "You wear good clothes!" They understood this to mean, "the good land"; and so the coast of North Carolina was called Wingandacon. They also understood the Indians to say that the Roanoke River sprang from a rock so near the "South Sea," that storms often dashed the waves into the spring from which it gushed, and that at this place there was an abundance of gold and precious stones. So Lane and some of his men set out to find the "South Sea," and continued their quest till they were forced to eat their dogs, to keep from dying of hunger. When they returned, they found the colony in great need and the Indians becoming hostile. At this critical juncture, an unexpected opportunity came for the settlers to return to England. In May, 1586, Sir Francis Drake touched at Roanoke Island with his fleet, and, yielding to the solicitations of the colonists, took them all back to England. They carried with them many interesting particulars about the nature of the new country, and much information in regard to the habits, manners, and government of the Indians, which had been collected by several learned and accomplished men who were members of the colony; but the greatest advantage that came from this expedition was the discovery of the Chesapeake Bay. It was in June that the settlers departed; and in the following August, Sir Richard Grenville came bringing for them fresh supplies, but found the island deserted. So he left fifteen men to hold possession of it; but these were doubtless slain by Indians, as they were never heard of afterwards.

The Lost Colony. — The settlement of Virginia was dear to Sir Walter Raleigh's heart; and in May, 1587, he dispatched another expedition, consisting of three vessels, which carried 116 persons, among whom were a number of men with their wives and children. Their plan was to found on the Chesapeake Bay a city to be called Raleigh;

but they were turned from their purpose, and landed on Roanoke Island, where they saw the bones of a man on the shore, and deer feeding around the deserted homes of the former occupants. They found the Indians bitterly hostile. This caused gloomy forebodings to fill their minds, and made them feel so strongly their dependence upon the mother country and their need of frequent aid from her, that, after several months had passed, they urged their governor, John White, to go to England for fresh supplies. To this he reluctantly consented, and in August, 1587, set sail, telling them that if for any reason they changed their location before his return, to carve upon some prominent object the name of the place to which they had gone, and above it a cross if they went away in distress. He left his daughter, the wife of Ananias Dare, who just a few days before his departure had given birth to an infant, christened Virginia. This was the first white child born in North America. He could have given no stronger pledge of his speedy return than he did in leaving his loved ones behind him. But in vain did the expectant colonists look for him. He found all England ablaze with excitement over the threatened invasion of the Spanish Armada. An attempt was made to send relief to the colony, but it proved unsuccessful; for the Atlantic was swarming with Spanish ships of war; and not till August 15, 1590, did Governor White again reach Roanoke Island. He found some tracks in the sand, and on a tree the word CROATAN, but there was no cross above it, and this seemed to indicate that the colonists had gone of their own accord to an Indian town called Croatan, which was on a neighboring island. White set out for Croaton; but, a fierce storm coming on, the captain of the ship *refused to* continue the journey and sailed for England.

Searching for the Lost Colony

When Sir Walter Raleigh learned that the colony was no longer on Roanoke Island, he manifested much anxiety in regard to its fate, and dispatched, it is said, five different expeditions in quest of the colonists; but no certain trace of them has ever been discovered. They simply disappeared from view. Had they become lost in the primeval forests and died of starvation? Had they been massacred by the Indians? Or had they joined the savages and, wandering off into the interior, become lost to civilization? These questions have never been satisfactorily answered; and this disappearance of over a hundred human beings constitutes a pathetic tragedy — the first of a long series connected with the history of our country.

QUESTIONS

1. Why is Virginia history so important?
2. What were the chief reasons England had for settling Virginia?
3. When did Columbus discover America? What points did he touch?
4. Who first discovered the mainland of North America?
5. Upon what did England base her claim to Virginia?
6. Who first tried to plant English colonies in America?
7. Who afterwards took up the subject of colonization?
8. From whom did he obtain authority to carry out his plans?
9. Where did Raleigh's first expedition land?
10. How were the explorers treated by the Indians?
11. Upon their return to England, what accounts did they give of the country?
12. How did the name of Virginia originate?
13. How were its boundaries described by an old writer?
14. By what other name was the Pacific Ocean known, and where was it supposed to be?
15. Give an account of Sir Walter Raleigh's first Roanoke Island colony.
16. Why did they call the coast of North Carolina Wingandacon?
17. What did they understand the Indians to say about the source of the Roanoke River?
18. What was the result of Ralph Lane's attempt to find the South Sea?
19. Who took the settlers back to England, and what information did they carry with them?
20. What was the greatest advantage that came from this expedition?
21. Give an account of the Lost Colony?
22. What did they urge their governor to do, and what agreement was made?
23. What pledge did he give of a speedy return?
24. What traces did he find of the colony upon his return?
25. Has its fate ever been known?

CHAPTER II

Renewed Interest in Virginia. — Nearly twenty years elapsed after the planting of the lost colony before another effort was made to settle Virginia. Then the times grew favorable for a renewal of the enterprise, and many influential persons became interested in it. Men, too, were found in abundance, who were eager to make personal trial of this new field of adventure. It seemed to offer an easy road to fortune and to renown. Fabulous stories written about America, its heathen peoples and " monstrous strange beasts," were read with delight; and maps, which showed the location of new lands, cities, and rivers, were eagerly examined. From the pulpit, clergymen declared that " Virginia was a door which God had opened for England."

The London and the Plymouth Companies. — Two associations were in 1606 formed to settle colonies in the vast domain known as Virginia. To Sir Thomas Gates, Sir George Somers, and others, who constituted what was known as the London Company, authority was given to found a colony in the southern part of Virginia, and it was to be planted anywhere between the thirty-fourth and the forty-first degrees of north latitude; that is, between what is now the southern part of North Carolina and the mouth of the Hudson River. Three years later, the boundaries of the southern colony were enlarged, and made to embrace the territory two hundred miles north and two hundred south of what is now known as Old Point Comfort and to extend "up into the land from sea to sea "; that is, from the Atlantic to the Pacific oceans. To the Plymouth Company authority was granted to establish a colony in the northern part of Virginia, afterwards named New England; but no permanent settlement was made in this territory till 1620, thirteen years after Virginia was settled.

The First American Charter. — On April 10, 1606, King James signed a charter, which he had himself prepared, for the government of the colony the London Company was to plant. The laws laid down were, on the whole, unwise, and not calculated to advance the prosperity of a struggling community. The chief provisions were as follows: The colony was to be governed by a council appointed by the king, the members of which were to reside in England; and this council was to appoint a subordinate one in Virginia, which was to govern according to laws, ordinances, and instructions prescribed by the king. The land was to be held free of any military or other service to the king, but to him was to be given one fifth of all precious metals that might be found. It was also provided that for five years the settlers should have things in common, but that after this land should descend to the eldest son, as it did in England; that the Church of England should be established; and that efforts should be made to find a short and easy way to the "South Sea" and to the East Indies. One provision is worthy of special notice — that the colonists and their children were to have forever the rights and privileges of native Englishmen.

The Beginners of the Nation. — One hundred men were soon secured, who were to be the pioneers. Among them were to be found men of every rank. There were some carpenters, laborers, and tradesmen, but more than half the number were gentlemen. Several of these were men of property, but many were younger sons, who went out from home in the hope of bettering their condition in life by a sudden accession of wealth. On the whole, the emigrants were not suited to bear the hardships of life in an uncivilized land. A few, however, had the qualities of leaders. These were Captain John Smith, who was a man of unusual ability; Bartholomew Gosnold, an experienced explorer, who was one of the most efficient promoters of the undertaking; George Percy, a brother of the Duke of Northumberland; and Rev. Robert Hunt, a minister of the Established Church.

Captain John Smith

The Departure. — Finally all preparations were completed, and on December 19, 1606, the expedition set sail from Blackwall, below London. The event stirred the patriotic feeling of England, and aroused great interest even in so busy a city as London. Michael Drayton wrote a lyric poem in honor of the argonauts, and prayers were offered up in the churches for their success. They embarked in three small ships, the *Susan Constant* of one hundred tons, the *Godspeed* of forty tons, and the *Discovery*, a pinnace of twenty tons. The expedition was under the command of Captain Christopher Newport.

The Voyage. — Captain Newport sailed round by the Canaries, following the usual route. Stormy weather made the voyage long and dangerous. For four months the ships were tossed and buffeted by the waves; and not till April 26, 1607, did the adventurers reach the Chesapeake Bay, the northern and southern capes of which they named after the king's two sons, Charles and Henry. Soon after passing the capes, they entered a beautiful river, which in honor of their sovereign they called the James, and a point of land at which they touched in entering its mouth, they named Point Comfort. The banks of this noble river, which the Indians called the Powhatan, were covered with showy white dogwood blossoms, mingled with brilliant red buds; and from either side the perfume of spring flowers was wafted to the ships. To the storm-tossed travelers the land looked like a veritable paradise, and they decided that "heaven and earth had never agreed better to frame a place for man's habitation."

The First Virginia Council. — The names of the first Virginia Council had been put, by orders of the king, in a sealed box, which was not to be opened till the expedition reached Virginia. It was examined on the night of April 26; and the councilmen were found to be Bartholomew Gosnold, John Smith, Edward Maria Wingfield, Christopher Newport, John Ratcliffe, John Martin, and George Kendall. Wingfield was elected president. But Smith was at first excluded from the Council on the ground that he had conspired to usurp all authority and make himself "King of Virginia." This charge was at a later period proved to be untrue, and he was then admitted.

Exploring. — Seventeen days were spent in exploring. The following quaint description tells what happened when a small party first landed: "At night, when wee were going aboard, there came the savages creeping from the Hills like Beares, with their Bowes in their Mouthes, charged us very desperately, hurt Captain Gabrill **Archer** in both hands, and a Sayler in two places of the body very dangerous. After they had spent their arrowes, and felt the sharpness of our shot, they retired into the Woods with a great noise and so left us."

Location of Jamestown Chosen. — On May 13, 1607, the settlers selected a site for a city, naming it Jamestown, which they fondly hoped would grow into a great metropolis.

The Settlement of Jamestown

The location chosen was on the western end of a malarial peninsula, lying on the north side of the river, about forty miles from its mouth. The peninsula has since become an island. The landing having been effected, the Council elected Mr. Wingfield president, who then delivered an oration, in which he explained why John Smith had been refused admittance to the Council. After this the colonists proceeded without delay to pitch tents, whose white coverings were soon seen gleaming among the green trees.

They rendered their arms and their provisions secure, and fixed a place to hold religious services. Later, cabins were built on the peninsula; and the place began to assume the appearance of a settled community.

A Fort Built. — Toward the end of May, as the men were planting corn, a shower of arrows came hurtling upon them, followed by the shrill war whoop of the savages. One boy was slain and seventeen men wounded. Up to this time but little preparation had been made for defense; but now all work was stopped till a strong fort could be built and palisaded. This was soon completed, and the settlers felt secure from attack.

QUESTIONS

1. What of the renewed interest in Virginia?
2. For what purpose were the London and Plymouth Companies formed ?
3. What parts of Virginia were given to each company?
4. By whom was the charter for the London Company signed?
5. What were the chief provisions of this charter?
6. Give an account of the pioneers of Virginia.
7. Name those who possessed qualities of leaders.
8. In what year did they leave England?
9. What interest was shown in their expedition?
10. Give the names of the three ships in which they embarked ? By whom were they commanded ?
11. Give an account of their voyage.
12. When did they reach the Chesapeake Bay?
13. After whom were the capes Charles and Henry named ?
14. What name did they give the river they entered?
15. Who constituted the first Virginia Council ?
16. Why was John Smith at first excluded ?
17. What is said of their explorations?
18. How did the colonists give the peninsula the appearance of a settled community?
19. What happened towards the end of May?

CHAPTER III

Early History of Captain John Smith. — Fortunately for the colony, it contained one man of remarkable ability — John Smith. He was born in Willoughby, England, his family being connected with the Lancashire gentry. By nature he was fond of adventure, and he lived at a period when the world was full of excitement and stirring deeds. Before he reached manhood he had fought in Flanders in the wars against Spain. In 1601 he enlisted with the Germans against the Turks. At the siege of Regal he slew three Turks in a tournament, and was honored with a triumphal procession. In the bloody battle of Rottenton he was captured by the Turks and sold into slavery; but he slew his master with a flail, and escaped into Russia. Then he wandered through Poland, Germany, France, and Spain, returning to England in 1604. Such, according to his account, were the leading events in his life before he came to America.

Visit to Powhatan. — While the settlers were trying to make themselves comfortable at Jamestown, Newport and Smith with twenty-three others sailed up the James to discover its head. They went as far as the falls of the river, and on the trip paid a visit to Powhatan, the acknowledged head of the Virginia Indians, whom they found in his royal wigwam, just a short distance from where the historic city of Richmond now stands. They were hospitably entertained by the savages; but Powhatan did not look with favor upon his guests, though he thought it best to hide his feelings. When one of his followers complained

Powhatan
(From an old print)

of the coming of the English, he replied that the strangers did not hurt them, but only took a little of their waste land.

An Unexpected Calamity. — Newport returned with his party to Jamestown the last of May, and in June he sailed for England, leaving a bark or pinnace for the use of the colonists. He had hardly taken his departure before an unexpected disaster befell the settlers. The marshy peninsula was full of malaria; and when July came, the men were attacked with such an epidemic of fever that at one time scarcely ten of them could stand. To add to their distress, the supply of food soon became insufficient, half a pint of wheat and as much barley boiled in water being each man's daily allowance. The noise of labor ceased, and no sounds were heard save the groans of the sick. At times as many as three or four died in a single night. Speaking of this period, Smith says, "Our drink was water and our lodgings castles in the air"; and George Percy wrote: "There were never Englishmen left in a foreign country in such misery as we were in this newly discovered Virginia." The facts show that this statement was not exaggerated; for by September half the men were dead, the brave Gosnold being among the number, and the remaining fifty in a deplorable condition, weakened by disease and by the lack of nourishment.

Half Survive. — When the supply of food had been exhausted, and the men were about to die of starvation, their wretched condition so moved the hearts of the sav-

Sickness at Jamestown

ages, that they gave them of their own fruit and provisions. Smith also obtained additional supplies by trading with the Indians and by intimidating them. The frosts of autumn brought health to the fever-stricken men; and now an abundant supply of food came from an unexpected quarter. Wild fowl appeared in large numbers, swimming upon the bosom of the river; and deer and other game came near the settlement. So the men feasted and half were saved.

Supposed Breadth of North America. — So little was known of the dimensions of the continent at this period that it was commonly supposed that the Pacific Ocean, or the " South Sea," as it was called, could be easily reached by sailing a little way up any of the rivers that ran from the northwest. 'To find a way to this sea was one of the objects set before the colonists by the London Company; for it was believed this would open an easy route to the East Indies, and pour out a golden tide of prosperity upon the shores of England.

Smith a Captive. — Complaint having been made that nothing had been done to discover the " South Sea," which had been the eager quest of so many of the early explorers, Smith, who was the leading spirit of the colony, sailed up the Chickahominy River to look for it. In the swamps of the river the Indians captured him, after which they set out on a march of triumph, exhibiting him to various tribes and spending their time in feasting. Finally they carried their captive to Powhatan, who was at Werowocomoco,[1] his favorite resort, which was on the York River, only a few miles from the historic field of Yorktown. The Indians, after holding a consultation, decided that Smith must die.

His Rescue. — Two great stones were brought, and the head of the struggling captive forced down upon them,

[1] Next to Jamestown, this spot is the most celebrated in the early history of Virginia. Its highly picturesque situation, overlooking the majestic York River, rendered it well worthy to be chosen by Powhatan as the seat of his power. Here the great Indian chief planned his schemes of conquest, and brooded over the disasters he feared would come to his people from the English. Here Pocahontas played as a child. It was here that Captain Smith, some time after his release, had a house built for Powhatan after the English fashion, the chimney of which is still to be seen, and is called to this day " Powhatan's Chimney."

while a number of warriors raised their clubs to dash out
his brains. But as they were about to strike, Pocahontas,
a dearly beloved daughter of Powhatan, then a girl about
thirteen years of age, rushed forward and, throwing her
arms around Smith, laid her head upon his to save him
from death. The stern heart of Powhatan was so touched
by his daughter's act that he spared Smith's life, and two

Rescue of Captain John Smith

days later sent him back to Jamestown, telling him that
he would in the future regard him as his son.[1]

Various Events. — When Smith returned to Jamestown,
he found the colony reduced to forty, and again in need
of food. But in January, Newport came with fifty additional emigrants; and another ship containing seventy more
arrived in May. These ships brought supplies also, and

[1] This is Smith's story of his rescue, and it has been doubted, but there is
sufficient evidence of its truth in all essential points.

Newport and Smith obtained corn by trading with the Indians. A fire at Jamestown early in the year destroyed much that the colony possessed, and progress was further delayed by a gold fever, which took possession of the men because they found yellow sand near Jamestown, a ship-load of which Newport carried to England.

Smith Explores the Chesapeake Bay. — Smith's active nature did not allow him to remain quietly at Jamestown for a long period. On June 2, he set out, accompanied by fourteen men, to explore the Chesapeake Bay. In an open boat, with no instrument but a compass, he traversed the whole of the Chesapeake on both sides. He not only did this, but also made frequent journeys into the interior, and opened communications with various tribes of Indians. As a result of these researches, he constructed a map of Virginia, which represented so correctly the natural outlines of the country that it was not superseded for many years; and even as late as 1873, it was referred to as authority on the disputed boundary line between Virginia and Maryland. When we consider the slender resources at Smith's command, the results he accomplished rightly place him in the highest rank among those who have enlarged the bounds of knowledge, and opened a way into an unknown land for colonies and for commerce.

Change of Rulers. — The first rulers proved incompetent. Wingfield was deposed by the people because he tried to seize the pinnace and escape to England, and Ratcliffe was made president. He was in turn deposed for bad management, and, in September, 1608, Smith was elected in his place. In times of adversity capable men always come to the front, and Smith was virtually the leader long before he became president. During the autumn and winter that followed his election he had entire control of affairs; and under his vigorous management, everything took on a better appearance. When food was needed he obtained it from the Indians, by fair means if he could, and by force when nothing else availed.

Promises that Could not be Fulfilled. — About the end of autumn, Newport came again, bringing with him another supply of emigrants, among whom were Mrs. Forest and her maid, Anne Burrus, the first English women that had ever settled in the colony. This time he had promised to do some impossibilities; for he had pledged himself not to return to England without obtaining a lump of gold, discovering the " South Sea," or finding one of Sir Walter Raleigh's lost colony. He was also instructed to crown Powhatan as a king acknowledging allegiance to England; and this he did, putting on Powhatan's head a tinsel crown, and giving him a scarlet cloak and other mock insignia of royalty. The haughty Indian monarch, in return for the presents he had received, sent King James a robe of raccoon skins and a pair of his old moccasins. The other undertakings Newport could not accomplish.

A New Charter. — In the summer of 1609, Captain Samuel Argall came on a trading expedition, bringing from England the news that Captain John Smith had been deposed. This proved to be true. King James had granted a new charter, which enlarged the limits of the colony and authorized the London Company to choose the English Council, and this Council was in turn to appoint a governor for the colony. Virginia was to have not only a governor, but also a lieutenant governor and an admiral; Lord Delaware, Sir Thomas Gates, and Sir George Somers had been elected to these offices, while Captain Newport had been appointed vice admiral.

The New Emigrants arrive, but the New Government does not. — Under the new organization, money enough was speedily obtained to send nine ships containing five hundred emigrants, to Jamestown. The fleet sailed from England in May, 1609, leaving Lord Delaware to follow, which he expected to do in a short time. To Gates, Somers, and Newport, commissions were given, authorizing the first one of the three that reached Virginia to administer the government till Lord Delaware arrived. The leaders were jealous of one another, and to keep one from securing an advantage over the others by a prior arrival, they all sailed together in the *Sea Venture*, the flagship of the vice admiral. In August, about three hundred of the emigrants, inadequately provisioned, arrived at Jamestown, bringing the news that the *Sea Venture*, containing the officers of the government and the rest of the party, had been lost in a storm.

New Settlements. — As none of the officers authorized to take charge of the government had arrived, Smith retained control of affairs. He induced some of the newcomers to settle at Nansemond under the command of John Martin, and others at the falls of the James River under Francis West, a brother of Lord Delaware.

Smith leaves Virginia. — While Smith was returning from a visit to the settlement at the falls of the James, he was severely wounded by the accidental explosion of a bag of gunpowder. Toward the end of September, when the ships that brought the emigrants returned, his enemies succeeded in having him sent back to England, charging him with having instigated the Indians to attack the settlers at the falls, because they had been insubordinate to him, and with plotting[1] to acquire a right to Virginia by

[1] See *The Beginners of a Nation*, by Edward Eggleston, pp. 37, 60, 61.

marrying Pocahontas, the daughter of Powhatan. Smith afterwards explored the coast of New England; but he never returned to Virginia. He died in London in 1631.

His Character. — The testimony of those who knew him shows that he was a man of action, craving restless movement, and taking pleasure in unremitting toil. He was fertile in expedients and full of energy, difficulties serving only to bring out the strength of his character, while his hopefulness under adverse circumstances enabled him to inspire others with confidence in him and in themselves. His researches in geography are unusually accurate for his times, and on practical subjects and colonization he wrote much that contains the highest wisdom. With all these strong qualities, he was at the same time so vain that, when he gave an account of his own exploits, his fervid imagination led him to color his narrative too highly. His character is paradoxical, and has to be studied in order to be understood. He has been called the "Father of Virginia"; and there is no doubt as to the great value of the services he rendered the colony.

QUESTIONS

1. What was the early history of Captain John Smith?
2. Give an account of the visit of Smith and Newport to Powhatan.
3. How did Powhatan regard his guests?
4. What calamity befell the Jamestown colony?
5. Why did the savages give them provisions?
6. From what source did the settlers obtain abundant supplies?
7. What was the supposed breadth of North America?
8. Describe the capture of John Smith.
9. Give an account of his rescue.
10. Upon his return to Jamestown, in what condition did he find the colonists?
11. Why were the first rulers deposed, and who was finally elected president?

12. Who were the first English women that emigrated to the colony?
13. What had Newport promised to do?
14. Give an account of the crowning of Powhatan.
15. When Argall came to Virginia, in 1609, what news did he bring from England?
16. What changes had been made in the government of the colony?
17. What officers had been appointed?
18. Why did John Smith remain at the head of affairs?
19. What new settlements did he make?
20. Why did Smith leave Virginia?
21. Give an estimate of his character.

REVIEW QUESTIONS

1. Give a general description of the Virginia Indians.
2. Describe their weapons, wigwams, and customs.
3. What was their method of warfare, and how did they treat their prisoners?
4. What is said of their education?
5. Describe their religion.
6. What is said of Powhatan?
7. Why did the English wish to settle Virginia?
8. Mention some early explorers and what they did.
9. Give an account of the early attempts at colonization.
10. Relate the story of the Lost Colony.
11. Why were the London and Plymouth Companies formed, and what territory was granted each?
12. What were the chief provisions of the first American charter, and by whom were they signed?
13. Mention some of the beginners of the nation, and describe their departure and voyage.
14. When and where did they make a permanent settlement?
15. Give the early history of Captain John Smith.
16. Give an account of his capture by the Indians, and his rescue.
17. Describe his last years, and give an estimate of his character.

CHAPTER IV

THE STARVING TIME — THE ADMINISTRATIONS OF DELAWARE, DALE, AND ARGALL

The Starving Time. — Disasters came fast after Smith's departure. The colony would not recognize the authority of George Percy, the acting president, and became divided into factions, each one of which had a leader. Francis West and a party of men who went in a ship to procure corn, sailed away, leaving the colony to its fate. The Indians renewed their hostility, and, filled with the determination to destroy the colony utterly, killed all who fell into their hands. Ratcliffe, who attempted to trade with the savages, was tortured to death by Indian women, and thirty of his men were slain. When the provisions were exhausted, the domestic animals were next consumed; and then the horrors of what is known as the "starving time" set in. During this period, one man deserves special mention as being apparently the only one who devised a plan to save the colony from utter destruction. This was Daniel Tucker, who built a boat and caught fish in the river, which, Percy says, "kept us from killing one another to eat." In six months the colony was reduced from nearly five hundred to sixty. The end was drawing near.

The Wreck of the Sea Venture. — There is no more romantic story in history than that of the *Sea Venture*, which is supposed to have suggested "The Tempest" to Shakespeare. The ship was wrecked on the coast of the Bermudas, which were at that time "accounted as an inchaunted pile of rockes and a desert habitation for Divels." " But all the fairies of the rocks were but flocks of birds, and all the Divels that haunted the woods were but herds of swine." This is what Sir Thomas Gates and his companions found to be true. They fared well, notwithstanding they had been shipwrecked, and " lived in such peace and plenty " that some wished to spend their lives there. But out of the wreck of the *Sea Venture*, they constructed with the aid of cedar timber found growing on the islands, two barges, which they christened the *Deliverance* and the *Patience*, and embarked for Virginia.

Wreck of the *Sea Venture*

The Rescue. — They reached Jamestown on May 24, 1610, just in time to save the remnant of the settlers. There was some talk of resuscitating the colony; but, when it was found that the provisions brought from the Bermudas would not last more than two or three weeks, they decided to abandon Jamestown. So on June 7 the whole party was crowded into the *Deliverance*, the *Patience*, and two pinnaces that were at Jamestown. The little fleet dropped down the river, and the next morning reached its mouth, where it met Lord Delaware, whose *ships were* just entering Virginia waters. The whole party ·

now returned to Jamestown, feeling that the hand of God had stayed their departure.

Administration of Lord Delaware. — Lord Delaware was the first executive officer in Virginia who bore the title of governor, and he came commissioned to rule with the sword of martial law. He maintained a mild but decided authority; and his influence for good was much enhanced by the virtues for which he was distinguished. He established regular hours for labor, tolerating no idlers but requiring the colonists to work during six hours of the day. Twice each day all had to attend brief religious services in the church, which was kept decorated with wild flowers. In every way he proved himself an efficient governor. He had the dwellings at Jamestown repaired, the forts garrisoned, and taught the Indians again to fear the English. But his health gave way under his duties, and, in March, 1611, he returned to England.

Sir Thomas Dale. — On May 10, 1611, Sir Thomas Dale came to take charge of the government, bearing the title of High Marshal. He received the appointment through the influence of Prince Henry, who took great interest in the welfare of the colony. Dale ruled by martial law with inhuman cruelty, putting offenders to death by torture, and even breaking one poor criminal on the wheel. Five men, captured in an attempt to escape to some Spaniards, who were reported to be near the settlement, were burned at the stake. A poor thief, for purloining a little oatmeal, was chained to a tree and allowed to starve. During Dale's reign of terror, no letters of complaint were allowed to reach England; and his administration, which came to an end in 1616, was known as "the five years of slavery." Dale lived in a cruel age, and he was a cruel representative of his age.

Results Accomplished by Dale. — Dale's administration had the happy effect of causing law and order to be properly respected, and it greatly advanced the material prosperity of the colony, though this was done by reducing the people to a bondage that was intolerable. He had much corn land cleared, and largely increased the number of horses, cattle, and hogs. One experiment which he tried produced results that proved to be important. He allowed each old settler to have a private garden patch of three acres, the proceeds of which belonged to him, while the rest of his labor went for the common good. From this it appeared that one man working for himself would make as much as ten men whose labor went into the public stock. This led at a later period to the private ownership of land, and the adoption of this system brought about great changes for good.

Argall. — Captain Samuel Argall now becomes prominent in Virginia history. In 1617, he was appointed lieutenant governor, and he had no sooner entered upon his duties than he proceeded to oppress the people under the cover of martial law, and to rob both the colony and the London Company, sending to England, while doing this, favorable reports of the condition of affairs. Cattle belonging to the colony he sold, and kept the proceeds. The Indian trade he carried on with the men and ships of the Company, and pocketed the profits. He plundered everybody with a pirate's rapacity, and even robbed Lady Delaware. When his high-handed proceedings became known in England, the London Company ordered all his goods and property to be seized. But Lord Rich, who afterwards became Earl of Warwick and took a prominent part in the Puritan movement, was Argall's · partner in England and, indeed, had secured his appointment as governor of Virginia. Now when he found that his confederate's downfall was certain, he dispatched a swift sailing vessel to Virginia, in which Argall escaped with his booty before the Company's orders could be executed.

QUESTIONS

1. What happened to the colony after Smith's departure?
2. Describe the starving time.
3. Who deserves special mention during this period, and why?
4. Give an account ot the wreck of the *Sea Venture*.
5. How were the survivors of the colony saved from starvation?
6. Why did they decide to abandon Jamestown?
7. Who first bore the title of governor of Virginia?
8. By what means did Lord Delaware accomplish much good in the colony?
9. Why did he return to England?
10. Who succeeded Lord Delaware?
11. Give an account of Dale's administration.
12. What was it called?
13. What good results did Dale accomplish?
14. What experiment of his proved important?
15. When Argall became governor, how did he act toward the people, and the London Company?
16. How did he escape with his ill-gotten gains?

CHAPTER V

POCAHONTAS

Her Friendship for the English. — The story of Pocahontas is one of the most beautiful connected with the early

Pocahontas

history of Virginia, and will always be read with interest by English people. She first appeared at Jamestown during the winter of 1607–8, bringing food to the colonists, who were in great need. After this she made frequent visits, attended by a train of Indians bringing baskets laden with corn and venison. In 1609, when John Smith was in her father's country trying to secure corn, she came at night and warned him of a plot the Indians had formed to kill him and his party; and when Ratcliffe and his men were slain, she saved one man and a boy from death. Many other acts of kindness are related of her, which show that she had a woman's tender heart, though she was an untutored savage.

Her Capture. — In 1612, Captain Samuel Argall went to the Potomac country to trade for corn. While on this mission, he learned from an old chief named Japazaws, that Pocahontas was in the neighborhood, and he conceived the idea of capturing her. So he bribed Japazaws to induce her to come on board of his sloop, which lay in

Marriage of Pocahontas

the Potomac River, and carried her off to Jamestown a prisoner, sending a messenger to Powhatan to demand, as a ransom for her release, the restoration of all English prisoners held by him, and the return of all arms and tools that had been stolen from Jamestown by the Indians.

Her Marriage. —Powhatan was not disposed to accede to these terms, and threatened war. But while negotiations were going on in regard to the occurrence, the matter was settled in a most unexpected manner. While Pocahontas was at Jamestown, John Rolfe, a young Englishman, fell deeply in love with her, and she reciprocated his passion. She professed faith in Christ, and was baptized under the name of Rebecca in the little church at Jamestown, from a font made of the trunk of a tree. Then she was married to Rolfe with the approval of her father.

The Cause of Peace. — To the colony, the marriage brought peace; for after it had taken place, Powhatan and the various tribes over which he had influence became friendly to the English. Even the Chickahominies, who were fierce fighters, were led by it to enter into an alliance, by which they acknowledged themselves subjects of King James, calling themselves New Englishmen.

Visits England. — Pocahontas lived happily with her husband, and with him visited England in 1616, when Sir Thomas Dale returned. Her arrival in London created a sensation, and all classes did her honor on account of her romantic history and the services she had rendered to the colony. She was presented at court by Lady Delaware, and was accorded the rank of a royal princess.

Her Death. — In March, 1617, she died at Gravesend, England, just as she was getting ready to embark for her native land, being only about twenty-two years of age when her eventful life came to an end. She left one son, Thomas, who was brought up in England. He married in London, but settled in Virginia, where he became a man of prominence, and where a number of his descendants are to be found among the honored citizens of the commonwealth.

QUESTIONS

1. What is said of the story of Pocahontas?
2. How did she show her friendship for the English?
3. Describe her capture by Argall.
4. What ransom was demanded of Powhatan for her release?
5. What unexpected settlement of the matter took place?
6. Give an account of the marriage of Pocahontas.
7. What benefit did it bring to the colony?
8. How was Pocahontas treated when she visited England?
9. When and at what age did she die?
10. Has she any descendants in Virginia?

CHAPTER VI

THE FOUNDING OF A STATE

The Crisis of Colonization. — The real crisis of colonization had now come. Dale's tyrannical administration and Argall's rule of robbery and ruin, had given Virginia such a bad reputation, that emigrants were no longer willing to go to a land where so many woes were experienced. One convict, who was offered the choice between transportation to Virginia and death by hanging, promptly chose hanging. The organizers of the London Company had hoped that they would reap large profits, as the stockholders of the East India Company were doing; but the colony had not proved a success financially; and it was now seen that commercial motives would have to become secondary, or else the whole scheme abandoned.

Triumph of Patriotic Motives. — Higher motives prevailed. "Divers lords, knights, gentlemen, and citizens grieved to see this great action fall to nothing"; and patriotic feeling was deeply stirred. The London Company passed under the control of a body of liberal statesmen, who put the founding of a state before the making of fortunes, and determined to adopt such means as were necessary to restore credit to the Virginia experiment.

The Great Charter. — Under the influence of such patriotic men as the Earl of Southampton, Shakespeare's friend, and Sir Edwin Sandys, the great advocate of popular liberty, the London Company on November 13, 1618, granted to Virginia a "Great Charter or Commissions of Priviledges, Orders, and Lawes." No copy of this charter is extant, but it is known that it limited the power of the governor, and provided for a legislative body to be composed of burgesses elected from the different settlements. This was the beginning of constitutional government in America; and the first House of Burgesses met at Jamestown on July 30, 1619, at the call of Governor Yeardley. The Great Charter provided also for an allotment of land to all settlers who were in the colony when Sir Thomas Dale took his departure; and so the oldest Virginia land titles date back to it.

Good Results. — In the spring of 1619, the people heard of the Great Charter and the changes it would bring, and they were filled with joy, feeling "now fully satisfied for their long labors, and as happy men as there were in the world." At the close of Argall's administration, the colony numbered not more than four hundred, but now emigrants came in large numbers. Twelve hundred and sixty-one arrived in the year 1619, and thirty-five hundred more within three years. All honor to such men as Sir Edwin Sandys, who founded in Virginia an English state with a constitution and a representative government, before England herself was delivered from the tyranny of the Stuarts.

Homes in the Wilderness. — When the founding of a state was made the first object, then the London Company became convinced "that a plantation can never flourish till families be planted, and the respects of Wives and Children fix the people on the Soyle." In 1619, Sir Edwin Sandys stated that the English in Virginia "were not settled in their mindes to make it their place of rest and continuance." During the same year, ninety young women were induced to emigrate to the colony. These found many suitors, as did others who came in later years. In 1624, the governor felt it to be his duty to issue a proclamation, threatening with punishment young ladies who betrothed themselves to more than one lover at a time. Happy marriages followed the coming of the women; and soon men began to look upon Virginia as their home. An

Young Women come to Virginia

interesting feature of these early marriages is that a man was required, after winning his wife's hand, to pay for bringing her to the colony in tobacco, which was then a costly commodity.

Introduction of Negro Slavery. — Almost simultaneously with the birth of free government came the curse of African slavery. In August, 1619, a Dutch man-of-war sailed up the James River, and sold to the settlers twenty negroes, who became the property of their purchasers and were made permanent servants. This was the beginning of an institution that was destined in after years to become fraught with harm. The traffic in negroes, when it had once begun, continued, but grew so slowly at first that thirty years after its introduction, the white population outnumbered the black fifty to one.

Indented Servants. — There was a class of persons in the colony known as indented servants. The term was applied to any one who was bound by a legal agreement to work for a prescribed time for another person. Some entered into an arrangement of this kind to defray their expenses in coming to Virginia, others were prisoners taken in war and sold by their captors into temporary servitude. It by no means follows that all persons of this class were of humble origin. Among them were to be found the sons of gentlemen. Some convicts were also· sent to the colony, but the number was small compared with the population; and the offenses committed by many of these had been of a political nature.

Friendly Intercourse with the Indians. — After Pocahontas married Rolfe, there had been peace between the English and the Indians. This had continued for so long a time that the Indians were no longer looked upon with distrust, nor did they display any hostility to the whites; and it seemed probable that the two races would continue to dwell in amity.

The Massacre of 1622. — In 1618 Powhatan died, and was succeeded by his brother, Itopatin, and he in a short time was supplanted by Opechancanough, a chief who was cunning, artful, and able. He at once formed a plot to exterminate the English, and for four years he schemed and planned, bringing tribe after tribe into the conspiracy.

To keep his design from being suspected, just before he
was ready to strike he entered into a treaty of peace with
the English. His plot was well conceived, his plan being
to fall upon all the plantations and settlements at the same
time, and by an unexpected blow to destroy the colony
utterly. The Indians manifested the greatest friendliness
for the whites up to the very time when the murderous
design was to be put into execution; and, even on the

The Massacre of 1622

morning of the fatal day, they came freely among them,
and in some cases took breakfast with the persons they
had planned to kill. At midday on March 22, 1622, they
swarmed out of their hiding places and engaged in a
wholesale butchery, sparing neither men, women, nor
children. By sunset 347 persons had been slain. But
the conspiracy met with only partial success. At some of
the plantations the settlers succeeded in beating off their
assailants. Jamestown and the places next to it received,

through a converted Indian,[1] warning in time to get ready for the danger that was impending, and when they were attacked, they easily put the savages to flight.

Effects of the Massacre. — The immediate effects of the massacre upon the colony were disastrous in the extreme. Many of the plantations were abandoned, and the alarmed people were crowded upon a territory so limited that it was hardly large enough to afford them a bare subsistence, and much sickness prevailed. In consequence of these hardships many became disheartened and returned to England, so that a year after the massacre, the number of inhabitants had been reduced from about four thousand to twenty-five hundred.

Retaliation. — The people were at first thrown into a panic; but they soon realized that they were strong enough to protect themselves, and entered upon a fierce though desultory warfare, which lasted for ten years. Before the massacre, it seemed probable that the Indians would, for all time, occupy the land along with the English; but by their treachery they lost the opportunity they had of retaining a part of their heritage in the territory of Virginia. They were now regarded by the whites as unworthy of receiving the treatment shown to enemies in civilized warfare, and were relentlessly pursued and shot down whenever opportunity offered. From this time on, the aboriginal inhabitants of Virginia were forced to retire from their homes and hunting grounds before the ever-rising wave of white settlers, and began, tribe after tribe, to fade out of existence.

---

[1] This friendly Indian was named Chanco. A tablet to his memory has been placed on the walls of the memorial chapel which was built at Jamestown in 1907 by the National Society of Colonial Dames and presented to the Association for the Preservation of Virginia Antiquities (page 89).

QUESTIONS

1. What brought on the crisis of colonization?
2. How was the London Company disappointed in its expectations?
3. What was the character of the statesmen who now obtained control of the London Company?
4. When was the Great Charter granted to Virginia ?
5. What is known of its provisions?
6. When and where did the first House of Burgesses meet?
7. What good result followed the granting of the Great Charter?
8. Why did Sir Edwin Sandys and the men that acted with him deserve special honor?
9. Of what did the London Company become convinced?
10. In 1619, what was said of the English in Virginia?
11. What was done to help matters?
12. What good results to the colony followed?
13. What was an interesting feature of the early Virginia marriages?
14. When and how was negro slavery introduced into Virginia?
15. What were indented servants?
16. Were all such servants of humble origin?
17. After the marriage of Pocahontas, how had the whites learned to look upon the Indians?
18. Describe Opechancanough's plot to exterminate the English.
19. Give an account of the massacre of 1622.
20. What were its effects?
21. From this time on, what became of the Indian tribes?

CHAPTER VII

TOBACCO

How regarded by the Indians. — Tobacco was growing in America when the first settlers came. The Indians regarded it as the gift of their Great Spirit, and planted it in their gardens along with their vegetables. To it they attributed many wonderful virtues. They threw tobacco powder into the air in a time of drouth to bring rain; tossed it upon the water to produce a calm when a tempest was brewing; and their priests cast it upon the sacrificial fires to propitiate evil spirits.

Introduced into England. — Ralph Lane and his companions, who learned to smoke it from the Indians, carried it to England. Sir Walter Raleigh, speedily becoming fond of it, introduced it among the nobility, and in a short time it became popular at the court of Queen Elizabeth. It is related that, as Sir Walter was sitting in his library, a servant, who came to bring him some water, saw smoke issue from his mouth, and hastened to pour the water over him, thinking that he was on fire. King James wrote a book against tobacco, and Parliament denounced it, but its consumption continued to increase in England till its smoke arose alike in the palace of the prince and in the cottage of the peasant.

The Foundation of Virginia's Prosperity. — Tobacco became the foundation of Virginia's prosperity. John Rolfe began the systematic cultivation of it in 1612, and it

64

became in a few years the universal crop. In 1617 it was seen growing in waste places in the streets of Jamestown, and even in the public squares. As the demand for tobacco increased, it became the chief source of revenue, and all other crops were neglected for it. Many persons of means settled in Virginia in order to raise it. It also rendered negro labor profitable, and thus encouraged the traffic in slaves.

Led to a Fondness for Country Life. — The cultivation of tobacco kept the population scattered. Each planter desired as large a farm as he could get, for it was discovered at an early date that tobacco grew most kindly upon virgin soil. This made it desirable that each plantation should contain a large area covered with original forest, so that as soon as the acres under cultivation became somewhat exhausted, new land could be cleared and substituted for them. This had a great effect in shaping the life of the Virginia people, for it tended to isolate the settlers, thus creating a fondness for the country and causing city life to be looked upon with little favor.

QUESTIONS

1. How did the Indians regard tobacco?
2. In what ways did they use it?
3. Who first carried tobacco to England?
4. What nobleman made it popular at the court of Queen Elizabeth?
5. What anecdote is told of him?
6. How was tobacco looked upon by King James and Parliament?
7. Who first began a systematic cultivation of tobacco?
8. What was the result of its increased production?
9. How did it encourage slavery?
10. What effect did tobacco have in shaping the lives of the Virginia people?

CHAPTER VIII

THE COLONY UNDER THE KING

Virginia Becomes a Royal Colony. — In England the struggle for Parliamentary freedom was going on, and the kingdom was divided between the Royalists and the supporters of Parliament. As a political measure, King James resolved to crush the London Company, because a majority of its members took sides against him. This he did, in 1624, by process of law. When the Company was dissolved, Virginia became a royal colony, and the king announced his intention of framing a code of fundamental laws for its government, but died in 1625, leaving this work unfinished. Charles I., who succeeded him, introduced no radical changes.

Lord Baltimore

Lord Baltimore. — In 1629 George Calvert, Lord Baltimore, a Catholic, though in no sense a bigot, came with a plan to establish, within the limits of the colony, a separate plantation as a refuge for persons of his belief. The people belonged to the Established Church, and were unwilling to see this done. There was a good reason also why they should be opposed to Lord Baltimore personally. He was the enemy and rival of Sandys, and had belonged to a faction in the London Company which had striven to

66

prevent the granting of the Great Charter; and now he came desiring to establish, for the promotion of his own interests, a colony of his people in the settled parts of the country. The House of Burgesses informed him that permission would be given to him to carry out his plan only upon condition that he would take an oath acknowledging that the king had supreme authority in religious matters. This he refused to do, and took his departure. But during his visit he found that there were no settlements on the north side of the Potomac River; and he readily obtained from Charles I., with whom he was a favorite, the promise of a charter to found a colony in that part of Virginia. Lord Baltimore died before the charter was issued, but his son planted the colony of Maryland. The Virginians made a vehement but unavailing protest against this division of their territory.

Opposition to British Encroachment. — Even at this early period, the Virginians began to appreciate their liberties as only a people who have known oppression can do. If we trace to its origin the unwavering opposition to British encroachment, which was manifested in later years, we find it had its beginning in 1624, when the House of Burgesses declared that, without its consent, no royal governor could levy taxes. In regard to other matters also, the people claimed the right to sit in judgment upon the acts of governors. This came out in the action they took in the case of Sir John Harvey, who was appointed by the Crown, in 1630, to rule over the colony. He was heartily detested by the people because he had sided with Lord Baltimore in the quarrel that had taken place over Maryland; and in his administration he was tyrannical, levied taxes that were unauthorized, and was unscrupulous as to the means he adopted to obtain money. So in 1635, the people shipped him back to England, sending at the same time commissioners bearing charges against him. The king reinstated the deposed governor; but the occurrence deserves a place in history as being the first open resistance to tyranny and vindication of constitutional rights that took place in America.

Sir William Berkeley Begins his Administration. — In February, 1642, Sir William Berkeley was appointed governor, and entered upon his duties at a period full of stirring events. He was about forty years of age when he came, and was for thirty-five years, with brief intermissions, at the head of affairs, holding office for a longer period than any other governor. He descended from an ancient English family, received his education at Oxford, had traveled extensively in Europe, and was "the perfect model of an elegant and high-minded cavalier." Soon after his arrival, he introduced some salutary measures which were very acceptable to the people, and thus his administration began auspiciously.

Opechancanough Strikes once More. — Opechancanough was still the ruler of the Virginia Indians; but he was now very old, and so decrepit that he could not walk. Neither could he see unless his eyelids were raised, as he had an affection which caused them to droop. But in his enfeebled frame the feeling of revenge still fiercely burned; and when he heard that the English were divided in the mother country, he decided that this was a favorable time to try once more to free his land from them. So in 1644, he rallied his braves for the last time and, falling upon the settlements on the upper waters of the York and Pamunkey rivers, slew about five hundred whites. But as soon as the English collected in force, the savages fled as they had done in 1622. Sir William Berkeley pursued

them with a body of horse, and captured Opechancanough. He was carried to Jamestown, where he was
kindly treated. But one of his guards basely shot him
in the back, and this caused his death. He was unsub-
dued to the last, and died as he had lived, the relentless
foe of the white man.

QUESTIONS

1. How and why did Virginia become a royal colony?
2. What was Lord Baltimore's plan to establish a settlement?
3. Who opposed it, and why?
4. On what condition did the House of Burgesses give their consent?
5. Did Lord Baltimore accept the condition?
6. What grant did he secure from Charles I.?
7. Who carried out his plans?
8. Against what did Virginia protest?
9. To what event can opposition to British encroachment be traced?
10. What action did the people take in the case of Sir John Harvey?
11. Which did the king sustain?
12. Why does this case deserve a place in Virginia history?
13. Who was Sir William Berkeley, and when was he appointed
    governor?
14. Give an account of Opechancanough's last attempt to exterminate
    the English.
15. What was the result?
16. Tell of his death.

REVIEW QUESTIONS

1. Give an account of the starving time, and tell how the colony was
   rescued.
2. Compare the administrations of Lord Delaware and Sir Thomas
   Dale, and give results accomplished by each.
3. Give an account of Argall's administration.
4. Relate the story of Pocahontas.
5. What is known of the "Great Charter," and what good results
   followed from it?
6. When was slavery introduced, and what were indented servants?

7. Describe the massacre of 1622, and give its effects on the people.
8. What is said of tobacco?
9. How and by whom was it introduced into England?
10. What influence did its cultivation have on the prosperity of Virginia?
11. How did Virginia become a royal colony?
12. Why did the people refuse to allow Lord Baltimore to make a settlement in their midst?
13. When did Virginia begin to show her opposition to British encroachment?
14. What happened in the case of Sir John Harvey?
15. Who was Sir William Berkeley, and when was he appointed governor?
16. Describe the massacre of 1644.

CHAPTER IX

THE COLONY UNDER THE COMMONWEALTH [1]

Execution of Charles I. — In England the struggle between the king and Parliament had grown so bitter that, in 1642, civil war broke out — the Puritan contest against royalty. The country was divided into two hostile parties. Those who supported the king and the Established Church were known as Cavaliers, while those who took sides with Parliament in its opposition to the king belonged to the Puritan party, and were known as Parliamentarians, or Roundheads. In all the strife that went on, Virginia had no part, but remained quiet and prosperous, though communication with the mother

Charles I

country was interrupted. The people were, on the whole,

[1] About a month after the execution of Charles I. the monarchy was formally abolished and a Council of State was appointed by the people. This body passed the memorable act which declared " that the people of England and of all the dominions and territories thereunto belonging are, and shall be, and are hereby constituted, made, established, and confirmed, to be a Commonwealth and Free State by the supreme authority of this Nation, the Representatives of the people in Parliament, and by such as they shall appoint and constitute officers and ministers for the good of the people, and that without any King or House of Lords." Oliver Cromwell was chosen " Protector " of the Commonwealth, which lasted from the execution of Charles I., in 1649, to the restoration of Charles II. in 1660.

royalists; and, as the difficulties that surrounded the unhappy Charles I. increased, they were filled with apprehension as to the result that would ensue. Finally their worst fears were realized, when the king was captured by his enemies, sentenced to death, and on the 30th of January, 1649, executed.

The Colony Loyal to Charles II. — The Virginians refused to recognize the authority of the Commonwealth, which ruled in England after the death of the king. The House of Burgesses met in October, 1649; and its very first act was to express the greatest respect for "the late most excellent and now undoubtedly sainted king." All reflections on his memory were declared to be treasonable, as were any doubts that might be expressed in regard to the right of Charles II. to succeed him.

The Coming of the Cavaliers. — After the king's cause had gone down in disaster, many Cavaliers fled from England to Virginia, where they were most cordially welcomed by the governor and by the people. Many persons of means belonging to the nobility, clergy, and gentry came over at this period. The importance of this immigration is shown by the fact that in 1650 Virginia contained about fifteen thousand inhabitants, and in 1670 forty thousand. The coming of the Cavaliers added to the loyalty of the people; for the exiles aroused sympathy by their misfortunes, and caused increased interest to be felt in royalty by the accounts they gave of the war that had been waged for the unfortunate king.

The Commonwealth Asserts its Authority. — For three years Virginia continued to acknowledge Charles II. as her sovereign; and, during this period, Parliament was too busy with affairs in England to give attention to colonies that were rebellious. But at the end of this time, it had triumphed over its enemies at home, and it then sent a squadron to reduce the Virginians to obedience. The ships reached Virginia waters in March, 1652, and found that Governor Berkeley had made preparations for vigorous defense. But, when negotiations were opened, the Virginians agreed to acknowledge the authority of the Commonwealth, provided their submission was considered as voluntary, it being understood at the same time that their country was not to be treated as if it had been conquered, but that the people were to enjoy all the liberties of free-born Englishmen, and should not be subjected to taxes without the consent of the House of Burgesses. Upon these terms a treaty was made between the Burgesses, who acted for the colony, and commissioners appointed by Parliament to represent the Commonwealth. When this took place, Governor Berkeley resigned, and was succeeded by Richard Bennet, one of the commissioners.

The Colony Prospers during the Time of the Commonwealth. — During the existence of the Commonwealth in England, which lasted from 1649 to 1660, Virginia enjoyed freedom of commerce with the whole world, and along with it came prosperity and a rapid development of the country. Many of the emigrants, who had poured into the colony during the civil strife in England and after the death of the king, were men of education and property, who now gave their time and energies to the care of their plantations. Virginia grew in reputation as a desirable place in which to live. The soil was so fertile, was so well watered by the many rivers, creeks, and brooks that coursed through it, and responded so easily to cultivation, that visions of limitless wealth were entertained as the result of new products, which, it was hoped, could be introduced. The gay-plumaged birds, the game that filled the majestic forests, the fish that were to be found in the waters, added to the attractions of the country, especially to the new settlers. It was declared to be "the best poor man's country in the world," and it was said, "If a happy peace be settled in poor England, then they in Virginia shall be as happy as any people under heaven."

QUESTIONS

1. What state of affairs in England led to civil war?
2. How did it affect Virginia?
3. What was the unhappy fate of Charles I.?
4. What was Virginia's attitude towards the Commonwealth?
5. Give an account of the coming of the Cavaliers.
6. What effect did it have on the loyalty of the people?
7. Why did the Commonwealth have to assert its authority?
8. Upon what conditions did Virginia agree to acknowledge its authority?
9. What did Berkeley do when the House of Burgesses signed the treaty?
10. What privileges and prosperity did Virginia enjoy under the Commonwealth?
11. Why was it declared to be "the best poor man's country in the world"?

CHAPTER X

The Restoration. — In May, 1660, Charles II. ascended
the English throne; and the event caused much joy in
Virginia. Even before the Commonwealth came to an
end, it is said that Sir William Berkeley invited the king,
who was living in exile in Holland, to come to the colony,
and raise his standard. From this, it is supposed, the
country obtained the name of "Old Dominion"; for it
was a place "where the king was king, or might have
been, before he was king in England." There is a tradition that Charles II., at his coronation, wore a robe made
of silk from Virginia, in token of his appreciation of her
loyalty.

Berkeley's Return to Power. — Early in 1660, when it
became evident that the end of the Commonwealth was
drawing near, the House of Burgesses elected Berkeley
governor; and the first act of Charles II., in regard
to colonial matters, was to confirm the appointment of
the stanch old royalist by sending him a commission.

Why Attached to Royalty. — This devotion to the king
seems inconsistent with the principles of popular freedom,
which the people had so cherished that they had almost
unconsciously developed a republican form of government;
but it must be remembered that their experience with royalty had thus far been encouraging; for under Charles I.

Coronation of Charles II

they had been practically independent, and during the interregnum, the Commonwealth left their liberties untouched. From Charles II. they had a right to expect the very best treatment; but they were doomed to bitter disappointment.

The Navigation Laws. — Parliament, in 1660, at the very first session held after the Restoration, decided to put into operation navigation laws to secure to England a monopoly of the colonial trade. These measures required that all tobacco exported from Virginia should be shipped in English vessels going to England, and that all foreign goods imported must be brought to Virginia in English ships. This policy stopped the free trade which Virginia had for some time enjoyed with the world, and worked the greatest injustice. When it went into operation, the result was that a ring of some forty or fifty English merchants had the whole trade in their hands, and reaped almost all the profit that came from the production of tobacco, fleecing alike the rich and the poor. Tobacco fell to a low price, while the cost of all imported goods was greatly enhanced. The colony sent Governor Berkeley to England to protest against the enforcement of these unjust laws; but he returned without accomplishing his mission, though he secured some very advantageous patents for himself.

The Royalists in Power in the Colony. — Even in Virginia a radical change took place after the Restoration. During the Commonwealth, the impulses for the advancement of the masses, which had been stirring England and the world at large, had been quietly at work in the colony, and had caused greater consideration to be shown to the common people, as is evidenced by the character of the colonial legislation that took place during this period. Now all this was changed; and it is not hard to see why it was so, if it be remembered that Virginia was but a part of England transplanted, and contained the same differences in society. The germ of an aristocracy had existed from the first settlement, and its rising power had been much increased by the emigrant royalists who came over during the interregnum. With the Restoration, this aristocracy came into power. A political revolution had taken place in Virginia, which proved fatal to many of the rights and privileges cherished by the people.

Oppressive Colonial Legislation. — The House of Burgesses quietly repealed the law which conferred upon the members a term of service extending through only two years, and thus legislated itself into an indefinite continuance of power. The government was now conducted in an expensive manner. All the officers received exorbitant salaries, and the people were heavily taxed to pay them. Oppressive taxes were levied also for other purposes, such as for arms and ammunition, to provide cannon and to maintain forts. The people could not see that the funds were always used for the purposes for which they were raised. They did see, however, that Governor Berkeley and his friends grew continually richer. Not only the taxes themselves, but the method by which they were levied caused the greatest dissatisfaction. They were laid, not on property, but on persons. They were poll taxes so heavy that they proved an intolerable burden to the poor, while the rich felt them but little. Religious intolerance came in also to increase the general discontent, laws being enacted which punished severely all dissenters. Finally, even political rights were abridged. In 1670, the right of suffrage, which for fourteen years had been enjoyed by all freemen, was restricted to freeholders and housekeepers.

Obstinacy of Berkeley. — In vain did the people protest that the Burgesses no longer represented them, and call for a new election. Berkeley persistently refused to dissolve a House which proved so subservient to his will, saying, in explanation of his refusal, that they were more valuable on account of their experience than new men would be. For twelve years complaints were sent to England against Berkeley, but they availed nothing. At last patience ceased to be a virtue, and there were indications enough that the people, exasperated by their multiplied grievances, were ready to rise against their oppressors; but Berkeley heeded not the mutterings of the storm that was gathering.

Criminal Prodigality of Charles II. — Oppression, unjust legislation, and robbery under the form of law were surely enough to exasperate a people so liberty-loving as the Virginians; but this was not all. The king, to whom they had been ever loyal, showed himself so utterly indifferent to their rights, that a large part of the population felt insecure in the possession of their homes. Charles II., while wandering in exile, soon after the execution of his father, had granted to a number of distressed Cavaliers the stretch of country between the Rappahannock and the Potomac rivers, known as the Northern Neck, by which act he gave to his favorites much land that had been long in cultivation. But now he committed an act that surpassed all others in prodigality. In 1673 he gave to Lords Culpeper and Arlington "all that entire tract, territory, and dominion of land and water called Virginia, together with the territory of Accomack," for the term of thirty-one years. All rents and escheats were to belong to them, as was the power to convey all vacant lands and, indeed, to manage matters in general as they wished.

Ready for Revolt. — When this act of the king became known, loud was the outcry raised against it. The whole population rose in protest. They had been loyal to the king in the past; but now they were only kept from breaking out in open rebellion by the efforts of influential men, who restrained them. The House of Burgesses in alarm dispatched envoys to England to bring about a change in the terms of the grant or else to buy it up for the benefit of the colony.

QUESTIONS

1. How was the news of the restoration of Charles II. received in Virginia?
2. From what incident is Virginia supposed to have obtained the name of Old Dominion?
3. What tradition is given in connection with the coronation of Charles II.?

4. By what authority did Berkeley again assume charge of the government?
5. Why was Virginia so attached to royalty?
6. Did she receive considerate treatment from the king?
7. What were the Navigation Laws?
8. How did the English merchants take advantage of these laws?
9. What action did the colony take, and with what result?
10. Under the Commonwealth, what advancement of the masses took place?
11. What change occurred after the Restoration?
12. Give an account of the oppressive colonial legislation.
13. Why did Governor Berkeley persistently refuse to dissolve the House of Burgesses?
14. What was the result of his obstinacy?
15. Why did the people feel insecure?
16. While in exile, what part of Virginia had Charles II. given away?
17. What was his crowning act of prodigality?
18. When this became known, what did the people do?
19. How did the House of Burgesses quiet them?

CHAPTER XI

Justice too long Delayed. — The king informed the envoys "that he was graciously inclined to favor his said subjects of Virginia," and promised a new charter for "the settlement and confirmation of all things," which he even ordered to be drafted; but notwithstanding the most persistent efforts made by the colony's representatives, it was so much delayed that before it was issued, a new cause of alarm furnished the people with what they desired — a pretext for appearing in arms in an effort to resist oppression by revolution.

Indian Troubles. — The Indians furnished the occasion for a popular uprising. In 1675, they began committing depredations and murders in some of the frontier settlements, and there were rumors that all the friendly tribes were about to break the peace that had existed for thirty years. There appeared, too, to be sufficient cause for such apprehension; for all along the border plantations prowling savages in blind fury murdered men, till the people became frenzied at the horrors of insecurity that hung over their homes. An appeal for protection was made to the governor; but he showed so little disposition to take prompt action that a suspicion was aroused that he secretly favored the Indians; and it was even hinted in explanation of his tardiness that he feared a war would injure the beaver trade with the savages, of which he had secured a monopoly for himself and his friends. Early in 1676, he did order out a force, under the command of Sir Henry Chicheley, to pursue the Susquehanna Indians who had slain thirty-six persons in the upper settlements of the Rappahannock and. Potomac rivers; but as the troops were about to set out, he suddenly changed his mind and had them disbanded. At last the people began to organize for their own defense; and soon after in the territory around the heads of the James and the York rivers, the citizens, including most if not all of the civil and military officers, tumultuously assembled and selected Nathaniel Bacon, Jr., as their leader.

The People's Leader. — Bacon was a native of Suffolk County, England, and was of. good descent, his family apparently belonging to the gentry. He was a cousin of Lord Culpeper, and his wife a daughter of Sir Edward Duke. He was educated at St. Catherine's College, Cambridge, where he entered in 1660, and took his M. A. degree in 1667. Reared during the stormy period of the Puritan contest against royalty, he had been influenced by the spirit of his times, and was animated by an ardent love of freedom rather than by an attachment to monarchy. He possessed natural talents of a high order, was eloquent as a speaker, engaging in manner, violent when excited, and recklessly brave. He had settled about the year 1672 on the upper James River, his plantation being one upon which murders had been committed by the savages. The high esteem in which he was held is attested by the fact that, though he had been in the colony only about three years, he had been appointed to a place in the Council, an unusual honor for one so young, for he was but twenty-nine. Such was Nathaniel Bacon, whom his countrymen enthusiastically chose as their commander, and well was he qualified for the office.

Other prominent leaders on the popular side were Richard Lawrence, a brilliant Oxford man, and Drummond, a Scotchman, who had been governor of North Carolina.

Declared to be Rebels. — Bacon's men collected their arms, and asked to be led against the Indians. But their

Bacon's Rebellion

commander, before complying with their request, applied to the governor for a commission, so that his acts might have the sanction of law. Berkeley did not send the commission; and so Bacon, in May, 1676, set out on his expedition without it, deriving his authority directly from the will of the people. But as he was on his way news reached him that he and his men had been declared to be rebels by the governor, and ordered to disperse. Some men of estates obeyed, but the rest continued on their way to the frontier and, after defeating the Indians, started back to the settlement.

Berkeley makes Concessions. — In the meantime the governor had taken vigorous action. He collected troops and, leaving Jamestown in haste, pursued Bacon; but he was suddenly stopped by the alarming news that all the lower counties along the James and York rivers had flamed out in rebellion under the leadership of Joseph Ingram and George Wakelet. Berkeley returned to Jamestown, and in view of the difficulties that faced him, decided to make some concessions. He accordingly dissolved the Burgesses, dismantled the frontier forts, which were the source of much complaint as being a useless burden, and in other ways showed a conciliatory spirit in the hope that he might keep the colony loyal to his authority.

A New House of Burgesses. — Berkeley ordered a new House of Burgesses to be elected, and the result was a surprise. The feeling of the people against the restriction of the suffrage was shown by the election, in some of the counties, of freedmen as burgesses. Bacon was unanimously chosen a burgess from his county of Henrico. The new House, which met early in June, represented the people, and a majority of the members were in sympathy with Bacon.

Bacon's Arrest and Apology. — When Bacon appeared to take his seat in the House, Sir William Berkeley did the only thing that he could do under the circumstances — arrested him. But he speedily paroled him, and an effort was made to harmonize matters. There was in the Council a near relative of Bacon, Nathaniel Bacon, Sr., "a rich, politic man." He, as was believed, induced Bacon, "not without much pains," however, to make a written apology for his acts. Bacon agreed to do this, his friends claimed, on the promise of a commission to fight the Indians. After he had thus humbled himself, he was pardoned by the governor, and restored to his seat in the Council. When this took place, many men from the upper country, who had hurried to Jamestown on hearing of Bacon's arrest, returned to their homes; and for a few days it looked as if the trouble was at an end.

Berkeley and Bacon

Bacon's Flight and Return. — If a commission was promised Bacon, none was ever sent to him. After waiting several days, he grew apprehensive that the governor's generous action in pardoning him was but a cloak to conceal his real purpose. Fearing that he would be arrested again after his friends had left, he fled from Jamestown, but in a short time returned at the head of about five hundred armed men. The House of Burgesses met in haste. The governor and his Council came out of the assembly room, and Bacon advanced to meet them. " Here, shoot me, 'fore God, a fair mark — shoot!" cried Berkeley. " No," Bacon replied, " may it please your honor, we will not hurt a hair of your head, nor of any other man. We are come for a commission to save our lives from the Indians, which you have so often promised, and we will have it before we go."

Bacon Before the Burgesses. — Bacon himself appeared before the Burgesses, and addressed them on the Indian troubles, on the condition of the public revenues, and on the grievances of the country. He was the next day appointed by the House commander in chief against the Indians, and this Governor Berkeley ratified. An act was passed pardoning Bacon and his followers for their proceedings, and a letter was even drafted to the king, highly commending them. The House also passed a number of salutary laws that were well adapted to reform abuses and to relieve the people; and to these Berkeley, who was for the time completely subdued, assented.

Berkeley Takes Refuge in Accomac. — Berkeley, finding that he could not depend on the support of the House of Burgesses, dissolved it, and then repaired to Gloucester, counting upon the loyalty of the planters there. He again declared Bacon a rebel, and, raising the royal standard, tried to rally the citizens to its defense. But he received only a half-hearted support; for, while the people acknowledged him as governor, they informed him that "they thought it not convenient at present to declare themselves against Bacon, as he was now advancing against the common enemy." The governor did not remain long unmolested, for Bacon, on hearing of the proclamation he had issued in Gloucester, abandoned the expedition against the

Indians, and marched to attack him. But Sir William hastily embarked in a small vessel and sailed across the Chesapeake Bay to the "Kingdom of Accomac," as it was called, which was regarded as a separate country, though it was controlled by Virginia.

The Convention at Middle Plantation. — At the news of the governor's flight, Bacon addressed a proclamation to the people of Virginia, inviting all who loved their country and their homes to assemble in convention and throw off the tyranny of Berkeley. The call was answered with alacrity. The most eminent men of the colony, four of whom were members of the Governor's Council, met at Middle Plantation, now Williamsburg, on August 3, 1676. The convention, after a stormy session, subscribed to an oath to make common cause with Bacon against the Indians, to support him against Berkeley, and even to resist any force that might be sent from England till the people's cause could be laid before the king. This oath was prescribed by Bacon, and it was administered by the lawful magistrates in nearly every county.

The Indians Defeated and Dispersed. — Bacon, now feeling sure of the support of the people, turned his attention to the Indians. He attacked and defeated the Appomattox tribe in the neighborhood of the present city of Petersburg, and then scattered the savages that were on the Nottoway, the Meherrin, and the Roanoke rivers. The Indian power was now broken, and Bacon disbanded most of his troops.

Berkeley's Return to Jamestown. — While Bacon was pursuing the Indians, Giles Bland, one of his followers, with a fleet of four ships sailed for Accomac to capture the governor. But one of the men turned traitor to Bacon's cause and gave up one of the ships to Berkeley, who then captured the others. After this stroke of good fortune, Sir William secured sixteen or seventeen sloops, and by means of this fleet transported his soldiers, numbering from six hundred to a thousand, across the bay; and on September 7, 1676, he took possession of Jamestown.

Destruction of Jamestown

Destruction of Jamestown. — When Bacon heard what had happened, he started at once for Jamestown, with such of his followers as he could hastily collect, and traveled "with marvelous celerity, outstripping the swift wings of fame." As he advanced, reinforcements joined him; but, when he reached Jamestown, his force was still inferior to Berkeley's. He prepared to cannonade the town; but Berkeley, evacuating it in haste, embarked with his troops on board the ships which lay in the river. Bacon entered the town; and, as his army was too small for him to leave a garrison in the place, after consulting with his officers, he decided to burn it so that it should no more furnish a refuge for the royalists. This was done on September 19, 1676, Lawrence and Drummond putting the torch to their own homes.[1]

---

[1] Jamestown was rebuilt, but suffered again from fire about twenty years later, and was gradually abandoned. Part of the church tower is all that remains of this ancient capital.

Death of Bacon. — Bacon now had all Virginia with him, and he was full of hope that he could establish for the colony a free government subject to Great Britain; but he did not live long enough to carry out any of his plans. During the siege of Jamestown he contracted a fatal sickness; and in October, 1676, he died at the house of Mr. Pate, in Gloucester. He was secretly buried by his faithful followers, and the place of his interment has never been discovered.

Collapse of the Rebellion. — At the news of Bacon's death there was widespread dismay; and a great change took place. There was no leader to succeed him; and his followers became broken up into separate bands, which Sir William Berkeley attacked and defeated in detail. The people grew weary of the desultory warfare that was carried on, in many cases, it appeared, only for plunder and revenge, and longed for the return of peace. Berkeley now exerted himself to encourage

The Old Church Tower of Jamestown
(Church itself rebuilt in 1907)

this pacific spirit. Finally, he entered into negotiations with Ingram and Wakelet, two of the most influential leaders, offering them full pardon if they would lay down their arms; and upon these terms they surrendered. Thus the rebellion which, in September, 1676, was triumphant everywhere, had, by the end of the year, fallen to pieces for lack of a head; and Governor Berkeley was again in authority.

Berkeley's Revenge. — Now that Sir William Berkeley was in possession of the government again, instead of adopting a policy calculated to heal the wounds of the colony, he displayed a spirit of revenge, which seemed to kill all humane feelings in his heart. He threw into prison many who had been prominent in the rebellion; and, knowing that when they were brought to trial they would be cleared by juries, he established martial law, by which men were condemned to death without fair trial, and then hurried off to execution.[1] Thus he brought about a reign of terror in the land, no man knowing when he might be arrested and hanged. Finally, after twenty-three executions had taken place, the House of Burgesses, in February, 1677, restrained him, by voting an address "that the governor would spill no more blood." "Had we let him alone," said one of the members, "he would have hanged half the country." "The old fool," exclaimed Charles II., on hearing of Berkeley's acts, "has hanged more men in that naked country than I have done for the murder of my father!"

Berkeley's Recall and Death. — Sir William Berkeley was recalled by the king, and passed out of office on the 27th of April, 1677. When he departed, the Virginians kindled bonfires and fired salutes, while a wave of joy passed over the land. On reaching England, he found that his conduct in Virginia was looked upon with horror by his friends, and that he was not sustained by the king. All

---

[1] Drummond was captured, and Berkeley, after telling him that he should be hanged in half an hour, had him executed in a very short time. Lawrence escaped from the colony and was never heard of afterwards.

this is said to have broken his heart, and on July 13, 1677, he died under a load of infamy, which dimmed the fair reputation he had won in his youth.

QUESTIONS

1. What did the king promise?
2. Did he send a new charter at once?
3. What cause for alarm now demanded attention?
4. Give an account of the Indian depredations.
5. How did Governor Berkeley treat the appeal of the people for protection?
6. Of what did they suspect him?
7. Finally, what action did the people take?
8. Who was Nathaniel Bacon, and why was he chosen leader?
9. What fact attested the esteem in which he was held?
10. Give the names of two other men chosen.
11. What request did Bacon make of Governor Berkeley?
12. Was it granted?
13. By whose authority did Bacon set out, and what news reached him?
14. In the meantime what action had the governor taken?
15. By what was he prevented from carrying out his plan?
16. What did he do now?
17. What was the sentiment of the new House of Burgesses?
18. Tell of Bacon's arrest and apology.
19. Give an account of his flight from Jamestown and return.
20. What did he demand from the governor?
21. On what subjects did Bacon address the Burgesses, and with what result?
22. Why did Berkeley dissolve the House of Burgesses, and repair to Gloucester?
23. What did he again declare Bacon?
24. What did the people inform Berkeley?
25. On hearing the governor's proclamation, what did Bacon do?
26. Where had Berkeley gone?
27. What proclamation did Bacon make?
28. Give an account of the convention at Middle Plantation.
29. To what did Bacon now turn his attention?
30. Tell of Berkeley's return to Jamestown.

31. Give an account of the burning of Jamestown.
32. What is left to mark the site of Virginia's ancient capital?
33. Tell of Bacon's death.
34. What happened when the people heard of his death?
35. How did Berkeley try to pacify them?
36. In what way did he seek revenge?
37. Finally what did the House of Burgesses have to do?
38. What did Charles II. exclaim on hearing of Berkeley's acts?
39. Give an account of his recall and death.

REVIEW QUESTIONS

1. Give an account of the struggle in England between the king and Parliament.
2. What was the Commonwealth of England?
3. How did it assert its authority in Virginia, and how did the colony prosper under its rule?
4. What is said of the restoration of Charles II. ?
5. What were the navigation laws, and how did they affect the commerce of Virginia?
6. Tell of the oppressive colonial legislation, and of Berkeley's obstinacy.
7. What is said of the criminal prodigality of Charles II., and to what did it lead?
8. Who was Nathaniel Bacon?
9. Why did Berkeley declare Bacon and his men rebels?
10. Give the leading facts of Bacon's Rebellion up to the convention at Middle Plantation.
11. What was done at this convention?
12. Describe the destruction of Jamestown.
13. Tell of Bacon's death, and the collapse of the Rebellion.
14. Describe Berkeley's revenge, and his death.

CHAPTER XII

FROM BACON'S REBELLION TO THE FRENCH AND INDIAN WAR

After Bacon's Rebellion. — The efforts of the people under Bacon to secure better government ended in failure. All the tyrannical legislation that had been enacted, in cluding the restriction of the suffrage, was put into full operation again; and freedom in the colony depended entirely on the royal will, except in so far as the inhabitants enjoyed the rights of Englishmen, which the common law accorded them. The rebellion was made a pretext by the king for refusing the liberal charter he had promised; and the one that was finally sent over was unsatisfactory, and did not contain a single political franchise.

The Tobacco Rebellion. — So dissatisfied were the people that they would have revolted again had not the disastrous effects of Bacon's Rebellion been fresh in their minds. As it was, small disturbances did occur, notably one which is known as the Tobacco Rebellion. This was partly the result of a law passed by the House of Burgesses to encourage the building of towns, which required ships to be loaded at specified places on the rivers instead of at the different plantations, the idea being that the observance of this law would render the erection of warehouses necessary, and that thus the foundations of cities would be laid. Many planters refused to obey the law, and, as ships were not allowed to touch at their wharves, they were prevented from disposing of their tobacco. This, together with the navigation laws, caused so great dissatisfaction that, in 1682, riotous proceedings took place; and in the counties of Gloucester, New Kent, and Middlesex, the planters destroyed a large part of the growing crop by cutting up the plants. The disturbances were quelled by the militia; and several of the ringleaders were hung. One, it is said, agreed to build a bridge, and on this condition was pardoned.

Governors not Interested in the People. — The royal governors who came and went during the period just after the rebellion showed, as a rule, but little interest in the people, and generally regarded their office as a means of advancing their own interests. One of the most avaricious was Lord Culpeper, who was appointed in 1675, but did not come to the colony till 1680. He sought perquisites of every kind, and endeavored to make the most money in the shortest time possible. Some relief came in 1684, when the Culpeper and Arlington grant was annulled and Virginia again became a royal province.

Good Effects of the English Revolution of 1688. — The English revolution, which drove James II. from the throne, because he violated the fundamental laws of the land, and endeavored to subvert the constitution, caused government to be regarded as a trust to be used for the benefit of the people, and not as an inheritance to be abused as a sovereign might see fit. The triumph of these ideas in England led, in a few years, to beneficial results in Virginia. The governors became less arbitrary, approved such legislation as was conducive to the good of the colony, and, in general, showed more consideration for the people. In 1690, when Governor Nicholson came to the colony, the people were on the eve of rebelling again, but he adopted a mild and conciliatory policy in accordance with the new views of government, and the danger of an insurrection gradually passed away.

The Coming of the Huguenots. — Toward the end of the seventeenth century, the persecution of the Huguenots on account of their religion began in France, and forty thousand took refuge in England. A number of them

William and Mary College

afterwards came to Virginia, where they found happy homes. Their principal settlement was at Manakin town on the upper James. These emigrants were brave, intelligent, and industrious. From them descended many distinguished families.

The Close of the Seventeenth Century. — As the century drew to a close, the people became much interested in the idea of having a college, where the young men could acquire the higher education which they were forced to seek in

England. The matter was pushed with vigor, and resulted in the founding of William and Mary College in 1693, named in honor of the reigning sovereigns. It was located at Middle Plantation, where five years later Governor Nicholson also founded the city of Williamsburg, to which he moved the seat of government. He designed that the streets of the new city should, when laid out, form the letters W and M as a compliment to William and Mary; but this plan was never fully carried out. When the century ended, Virginia had a population of seventy thousand, and was rapidly advancing in prosperity and importance.

Alexander Spotswood. — In 1710, the illustrious Colonel Alexander Spotswood, a gallant officer, who had served under Marlborough, and had been wounded in the famous battle of Blenheim, was appointed governor. He was in the prime of manhood, courteous in manner, active and enterprising in nature. He met with a most cordial welcome, and he brought a formal confirmation of the writ of *habeas corpus*,[1] a right cherished by the people. Governor Spotswood had the welfare of the colony at heart, and exerted himself to develop its resources. He established the first iron furnaces ever located in America, and on account of this he was called the "Tubal Cain" of Virginia.

Spotswood Crosses the Blue Ridge. — A few years after he reached the colony, a love of adventure filled him with the desire to penetrate the country beyond the Blue Ridge, which had been supposed for a long time to present a barrier forever impassable to men. In 1716, he with a number of his companions, well mounted and attended by "rangers, pioneers and indians," set out on a

---

[1] The object of the writ of *habeas corpus* is to prevent unjust imprisonment, the literal meaning of the words being "you may have the body."

journey of exploration. They succeeded in ascending the range, and on its top drank the health of the king, after which they went down into the beautiful valley, naming the river running through it, which we now call the Shenandoah, the Euphrates. Spotswood, to commemorate his triumph, presented to his companions small golden horseshoes, set with garnets and other jewels inscribed with the motto, "Sic juvat transcendere montes."[1] From this incident the order of the "Knights of the Golden Horseshoe" originated. Spotswood ceased to be governor in 1722; but he spent the remainder of his days in Virginia,[2] where his memory is much honored and where many of his descendants still live.

Richmond and Petersburg Founded. — In 1733, Colonel William Byrd[3] laid the foundation of two new cities at places "naturally intended for Marts." These he named

[1] Thus it is a pleasure to cross the mountains.

[2] Spotswood lived at the old town of Germanna in Spotsylvania County. Colonel Byrd narrates the following interesting incident of a visit he made to the ex-governor in 1732. "Here I arrived about three o'clock, and found only Mrs. Spotswood at home, who received her old acquaintance with many a gracious smile. I was carried into a room elegantly set off with pier-glasses, the largest of which came soon after to an odd misfortune. Among other favorite animals that cheered this lady's solitude, a brace of deer ran familiarly about the house, and one of them came to stare at me as a stranger. But unluckily spying his own figure in the glass, he made a spring over the tea-table that stood under it, and shattered the glass to pieces, and falling back upon the tea-table made a terrible fracas among the china. This exploit was so sudden, and accompanied with such a noise, that it surprised me, and perfectly frightened Mrs. Spotswood. But it was worth all the damage to see the moderation and good humor with which she bore the disaster."

[3] William Byrd (1674-1744), born at Westover, Va., was the first native author. He was educated in England, and was a member of the Royal Society. Returning to Virginia, he was made receiver-general of revenues, was then appointed public agent to the Court and Ministry of England. He was also president of the Council of the colony. His writings show much wit and culture.

Richmond and Petersburg; and they soon grew into substantial towns. The *Virginia Gazette*, the first newspaper that appeared in the colony, was issued in Williamsburg i 17.. ; and its columns contained an advertisement invi ... everybody to come and live at Richmond.

Settlement of the Valley. — The people of Virginia mad their homes first near the seacoast, along the lowland river Up these they gradually extended their settlements til about a hundred years after the founding of Jamestow they had reached the mountains. These, Spotswood ha shown were not impassable; and so some years later wave of population from the lowlands began to cross th mountains and to pour itself into the fertile Shenandoa valley. Just before this happened, a tide of immigratio from Pennsylvania had come into the lower valley. Thi consisted of Scotch-Irish and Germans, who had bee drawn to the country by rumors of its many advantage: These early settlers of the valley were of excellent mat rial to make good citizens. The history of the Scotcl Irish in America has never been fully written. Whe this is done, it will appear that their immigration was ne in importance to the coming of the Cavaliers to Virgini and the Puritan migration to New England, so great ha been its influence.

QUESTIONS

1. What was the condition of the colony after Bacon's Rebellion?
2. What was the Tobacco Rebellion?
3. How did the royal governors regard the people?
4. In what manner did Lord Culpeper treat the people?
5. Relief came in what way?
6. How was the English revolution of 1688 beneficial to Virginia?
7. What policy did the government adopt, and with what result?
8. Who were the Huguenots, and why did they come to Virginia?
9. When and where was William and Mary College founded?

10. What city was founded at the same place?
11. Describe Governor Nicholson's design for the streets.
12. What population did Virginia have at the close of the seventeenth century?
13. Who was Alexander Spotswood, and how was he received?
14. What legal right did he bring to the people?
15. What did he establish in Virginia?
16. Give an account of Spotswood's crossing the Blue Ridge.
17. What did they do on reaching the summit, and how did they commemorate the event?
18. When and by whom were the cities of Richmond and Petersburg founded?
19. What invitation did the *Virginia Gazette* give to the public?
20. Give an account of the gradual settlement of the valley of Virginia.
21. Of what nationality were its settlers?

CHAPTER XIII

THE FRENCH AND INDIAN WAR

The Question of Supremacy. — The rivalry existing between France and England, which had caused so many bloody wars in Europe, was transferred also to America. Both had planted extensive colonies; and, as these grew, their interests came into conflict. Which nation was to rule in the New World? This question had to be decided; and as the middle of the eighteenth century drew near, it was evident that the settlement was not far off.

The Plan of France. — The French had secured possession of the two great rivers of the country, the Mississippi and the St. Lawrence. They had Canadian France in the north and Louisianian France in the south; and they conceived the bold idea of connecting these settlements. So they built a line of forts which ran from Quebec to the Great Lakes, and then down the Illinois and the Mississippi rivers to the Gulf of Mexico. Thus they planned to hem the English colonies in on the Atlantic, and not to allow them to extend themselves further toward the west.

The English Plan. — The English suddenly awoke to the fact that they were about to lose the heart of the continent, and decided to colonize the rich country west of the Alleghany Mountains. For this purpose the Ohio Company was formed; and in 1752, it received a grant of half a million acres of land on the east bank of the upper

Ohio — the territory now contained in West Virginia and southwest Pennsylvania.

Protest from Virginia. — The French watched the movement the English were making, and decided to stop it by building a new line of forts from Lake Erie to the head of inland navigation — the point where the Alleghany River joins with the Monongahela to form the Ohio. In carrying out this plan, they proposed without ceremony to possess themselves of territory that belonged to Virginia.

When this design was suspected, Robert Dinwiddie, who was then governor, resolved to send a messenger to M. de St. Pierre, the French commander, who was at a fort about fifteen miles south of Lake Erie, to inform him that the territory on the Ohio belonged to Virginia, and to protest against any invasion of it.

George Washington

The Envoy Selected. — For the discharge of this duty, Governor Dinwiddie selected a native Virginian, George Washington, who was destined to fill a prominent place in the history of his country. He was born in Westmoreland County on February 22, 1732, and descended from a family that belonged to good English stock. His father died when he was but ten years old, and so he had learned at an early age to rely upon himself. Though he had received but a common school education, yet he had made the best use of his opportunities; and when sixteen years old had been engaged by Lord Fairfax to survey land he owned across the Blue

Ridge. This led to a lifelong friendship between the two men; and Washington doubtless derived much benefit from his association with Fairfax, who had grown up in the most elegant society in London. Washington in all his actions during his boyhood and early manhood had borne the highest reputation for judgment, administrative ability, and integrity of moral character. He was just twenty-one when he set out on his dangerous mission.

The Journey and the Result. — The journey was full of perils and hardships; but finally Washington reached his destination. M. de St. Pierre received him most courteously; but, when he read Dinwiddie's letter, he sent back the reply that, in all he had done, he had been acting under the instructions of the governor of Canada, and that he should continue to obey orders, as was the duty of a soldier. With this unsatisfactory answer, Washington was forced to return. His journal giving an account of his expedition, which was published both in Virginia and in England, first unfolded the hostile intentions of the French. It was now seen that their encroachments could only be stopped by an appeal to arms, which would involve a contest with the Indians also, for they had formed an alliance with the French.

The Opening of Hostilities. — In January, 1754, a company of Virginia pioneers, less than fifty in number, took possession of the forks of the Ohio River, where Pittsburg now stands, which was the strategic point of the whole disputed territory, and commenced building a fort. But in April they were dispersed by the French, who completed the stronghold, and named it Fort Duquesne, in honor of the nobleman who was governor of Canada. In the meantime Virginia had equipped a small force which, under the command of Washington, was pushing on toward the forks of the Ohio. But, on the way, Washington learned that the French had already secured possession of the coveted position. He continued his march, however, till he reached a place called Great Meadows, about forty miles distant from Fort Duquesne, where he met and defeated a small French force. He then halted and built Fort Necessity. This the French besieged and captured, but allowed Washington and his men to march back to Virginia.

England sends General Braddock to Virginia. — The affair at Great Meadows caused the English government to take vigorous action. Early in 1755, one thousand of the king's regular troops were sent over, first to capture Fort Duquesne and after this other French forts toward the Great Lakes. These were under the command of General Edward Braddock, who was a brave man; but he made the fatal mistake of supposing that war could be carried on with success in an American wilderness on the same plan as upon the plains of Europe. Warnings were repeatedly given him that he had to fight, not only the French, but also the Indians, whose peculiar method of warfare, added to the wild character of the country, gave them an advantage over regular troops, and made them an enemy to be feared. To Benjamin Franklin, who spoke to him of the danger he would have to guard against from this source, he replied impatiently, "These savages may be indeed a formidable enemy to raw American militia, but upon the king's regular and disciplined troops, sir, it is impossible to make any impression."

Braddock's Defeat. — Some time was consumed in preparations; but finally the army, reinforced by about one thousand colonial soldiers, began to move toward Fort Duquesne, Braddock confident that an easy victory was before him. In July the army crossed the Monongahela River, at a point about ten miles from the fort, where it was attacked by a force of Canadians and Indians, and literally cut to pieces. Half the English fell, killed or wounded, and the remainder fled panic-stricken toward Virginia. General Braddock received a mortal wound, from the effects of which he died. Washington, who had accompanied the expedition as a member of Braddock's staff, put himself at the head of the colonial troops, and covered the retreat of the regulars as far as was possible. Thus the campaign that was to accomplish so much ended in dire disaster.

Predatory Inroads on the Frontier. — The whole western frontier of Virginia was now unprotected.   The Indians in the country toward the Ohio, encouraged by the success that attended their arms in the contest with Braddock, began boldly to attack the frontier, and even advanced as far as the neighborhood of Winchester, their line of march being always marked by murders and outrages of the most blood-curdling kind.

Virginia Defends her Frontiers. — The House of Burgesses raised and equipped additional forces which were put under the command of Washington, who was so much distressed by the conditions confronting him that, while at Winchester, he wrote Governor Fauquier a letter in which he said: "The supplicating tears of the women and moving petitions of the men melt me into such deadly sorrow that I solemnly declare, if I know my own mind, I could offer myself a willing sacrifice to the butchering enemy, provided that would contribute to the people's ease." He exerted himself to the utmost to stop the atrocities of the savages, building a fort at Winchester and others along the border, to which the distressed inhabitants could fly for refuge; and he met with a wonderful degree of success in his efforts, when the limited supply of men and means at his command are taken into consideration.

End of the War. — For some time, in the struggle that was going on, success seemed about to rest with the French; but in 1758, the English began to prosecute the war more vigorously. During this year another expedition, under the command of General John Forbes, was sent against Fort Duquesne. His army numbered about six thousand, sixteen hundred of whom were Virginians under Washington. This time the Virginians led the advance. On the approach of the army, the French blew up the fort and retreated. This event brought the worst of the border troubles to an end, though the Indians continued to commit occasional outrages for some time. The following year, the English captured Quebec, which virtually decided the contest. A few years later France yielded her possessions east of the Mississippi River to England.

QUESTIONS

1. Give an account of the rivalry existing between France and England.
2. What was now the question to be decided?
3. Give the plan adopted by France.
4. The English plan.
5. How did the French decide to stop the English?
6. What message did the governor of Virginia send the French commander?
7. Who was George Washington, when and where born?
8. What led to a lifelong friendship between Washington and Lord Fairfax?
9. What is said of his character?
10. Give an account of his journey, and of its result.
11. Tell of the opening of hostilities.
12. What happened at Great Meadows?

13. Whom did the English send to capture Fort Duquesne, and wha fatal mistake did he make?
14. On being warned by Benjamin Franklin, what was his reply?
15. Tell of Braddock's defeat.
16. Who then took the head of the colonial troops?
17. Encouraged by this victory, what did the Indians do?
18. What was the letter Washington wrote to Governor Fauquier?
19. In what way did he try to stop the atrocities of the savages?
20. In what year did Fort Duquesne fall into the hands of the English
21. How did the war end?

CHAPTER XIV

COLONIAL LIFE

Its Golden Age. — In the eighteenth century, colonial life had passed through the formative period, and reached the full flower of its development. The settlers in the Valley, it is true, were still undergoing the hardships of pioneer life; but in eastern Virginia, along the rivers, a prosperous people lived in luxury and security. Before entering upon the stirring events of the Revolution, it will be interesting to take a brief glance at Old Dominion society in the good old days when life was easy and men were happy.

A Pioneer

Classes that formed Society. — Society was composed of a number of classes. There were the large planters and the small planters, both owning land and slaves. The line between these classes was not clearly marked, for they shaded into one another. They dwelt harmoniously together, and stood shoulder to shoulder in any time of public need. There was also, to some extent, a separate class, made up of men who were called overseers, because they were employed by large land owners to overlook their servants and their property. Many of these became themselves land owners and the holders of slaves. Mention must also be made of still another class, composed of the descendants of indented servants and of convicts. They were ignorant, indolent, and turbulent, but were few in number, and were unimportant both socially and politically. These various classes, with the negroes, who were rapidly increasing in numbers, constituted the different elements of Old Virginia society.

Life on a Large Plantation. — Each large plantation was a little community, which produced nearly everything needed for its own use. It furnished not only food for all who dwelt upon it, but also the raw materials out of which clothes, shoes, and the various articles for common use were manufactured. All the work was done by negroes, under the supervision of their masters, mistresses, or overseers.[1]

Life of the Planter. — It is evident that the planter, who had such varied interests to look after did not, as a rule, live a life of idleness and ease, as has often been stated. It is true that he had his amusements, horse-racing, fish-

[1] The various operations that were carried on upon a large plantation are well described by General John Mason as follows: "Thus my father had among his slaves carpenters, coopers, sawyers, blacksmiths, tanners, curriers, shoemakers, spinners, weavers, and knitters, and even a distiller. His woods furnished timber and plank for the carpenters and coopers, and charcoal for the blacksmith; his cattle, killed for his own consumption and for sale, supplied skins for the tanners, curriers, and shoemakers; and his sheep gave wool, and his fields produced cotton and flax for the weavers and spinners, and his orchards fruit for the distiller."

ing, hunting, and chasing the fox, being his favorite sports; but the greater part of his time, he spent in superintending the different operations which took place

upon his estate, and in look-ing after the welfare of all the people who lived on it. He dispensed a most gen-erous hospitality to his friends and to strangers, keeping open house for all who came. This was ren-dered easy by a large reti-nue of servants and by the abundant supplies of food which the plantation fur-nished. The free enter-tainment of guests was so common that, in the seven-teenth century, a law was passed requiring even an innkeeper, if he wished to

Virginia Hospitality

charge for food and shelter, to notify a guest upon his arrival; otherwise he could not make him pay anything.

Life of a Planter's Wife. — Domestic affairs occupied to a great extent the time of the mothers and daughters of a household. Needlework that knew no end, the training of servants, and looking after the general affairs of the establishment, were the monotonous but useful occupa-tions of the Virginia women. Toward the end of the eighteenth century, a visitor to Mount Vernon says that she found Mrs. Washington in a room nicely fixed for all kinds of work. She then continues: "On one side, sits the chamber maid, with her knitting; on the other, a little

coloured pet, learning to sew.   An old, decent woman is
there, with her table and shears, cutting out the negroes'
winter clothes, while the good old lady (Mrs. Washington) directs them all, incessantly knitting herself.   She
points out to me several pairs of nice coloured stockings
and gloves she had just finished, and presents me with

In a Virginia Home

a pair half done, which she begs I will finish and wear
for her sake."[1]   Bishop Meade, in commenting on this
description says: "If the wife of General Washington,
having her own and his wealth at command, should thus
choose to live, how much more the wives and mothers
of Virginia with moderate fortunes and numerous chil—
dren."

[1] See *Old Churches and Families of Virginia.*   Vol. I, p. 98.

The "Great House." — The dwelling house on a large plantation was known as the manor house, or the "great house." It was not necessarily large, but its name originated from the contrast it presented to the other buildings on the place. In the seventeenth century, the typical dwelling was a framed building of moderate size, possess-

A Manor House

ing more width than depth, and having usually a chimney at each end. Many houses were, however, built of brick, and some of stone. For a long time, the dwellings displayed but little architectural beauty; but, during the eighteenth century, when the planters had grown wealthy, a number of elegant residences, resembling those of the English gentry were erected. Some of these were square or nearly so, two stories or more high, had deep cellars, large rooms, broad halls, and rejoiced in great fireplaces. If there was an overseer on the plantation, he dwelt in a separate house, which was less pretentious than the "great house" in appearance.

Furniture. — The furniture was generally imported, and that used by the better classes was usually of mahogany, or else made of less costly material, covered with thin strips of mahogany called veneer. The bedsteads were so high that frequently steps were needed to reach them. They had tall posts, and were inclosed by curtains. Underneath them, trundle-beds, which were used for the children of the family, were kept during the day. These were hid from view by narrow curtains. The rich man's spoons were of silver, those of the poor man of iron or pewter. Dishes and plates were made of earthenware or pewter. Knives were of steel,

Colonial Furniture

but forks were not in general use till the eighteenth century. A treadle wheel for spinning flax, a large wheel for spinning wool, and a hand-loom for weaving cloth were common household articles.

The Kitchen. — The kitchen was some distance from the "great house," and its most striking feature was a fireplace, sometimes twelve feet wide. The cooking utensils were iron pots, gridirons, kettles, saucepans, frying pans, etc. As each article of food was cooked in a separate vessel, it possessed an individual flavor that is unknown in cooking that comes from the stoves and ranges of the present day.

Food. — The hardships of pioneer days were gone; and, in no part of the world was a more bountiful supply of food of various kinds to be found than in Virginia. There were beef, pork, venison, mutton to a limited extent, game of all kinds, vegetables and fruits to suit every taste. Such viands as they were, prepared in the homes of the better classes, could not fail to please the most fastidious.

The Negro Quarters. — The negroes dwelt together in a settlement which presented the appearance of a village, the houses of which were of the plainest kind, built of logs or undressed planks. Each cabin, however, contained furniture enough to make the occupants comfortable. As a rule the negroes were well fed and well clothed; and it cannot be said that they were an unhappy race. Free from all the responsibilities of life, they brought up large families, and enjoyed to the fullest extent such blessings as came to them.

Relation of Master and Servant. — In the olden times, the negroes were usually called servants, not slaves. They were generally kindly treated, though there were exceptional cases of cruelty to them; and it was by no means uncommon for genuine affection to exist between a master and his servants. Bruce, in his *Economic History of Virginia,*[1] says: "There is no reason to doubt that the planters were as a body just and humane in their treatment of their slaves. The solicitude · exhibited by John Page of York was not uncommon; in his will he instructed

---

[1] The reader who wishes full information in regard to colonial life is referred to Bruce's *Economic History of Virginia in the Seventeenth Century*, a most admirable and scholarly work.

his heirs to provide for the old age of all the negroes who descended to them from him, with as much care in point of food, clothing, and other necessaries, as if they were still capable of the most profitable labor."

Dress. — The wealthy planter showed a child's fondness for ornamentation; and he had an opportunity to gratify his taste when the frequent gatherings of friends took place at his home, at Christmas, at weddings, and when he attended services at the parish church. On such occasions, with his bright-colored coat and breeches, made frequently of plush, with his embroidered waistcoat, his long silk stockings, silver buttons and shoe-buckles, his ruffled shirt, and his head adorned with a flowing wig, he presented an appearance that was truly gorgeous. But his wife was fully his equal; for she was apt to appear in crimson satin bodice trimmed with point lace, a petticoat of rich, black oriental silk, costly shoes, and silk hose.

Education. — Primary education was given in the "old field" schools, where the three R's were taught, and perhaps something more. There were some private academies also; but the higher education had to be sought in England till William and Mary College was founded, and so was denied to all except the sons of the rich in the early days.

Roads. — For a long time the numerous creeks and rivers, which traverse the country, furnished the only highways for trade and also for travel. There were but few roads till late in the eighteenth century. Travel across the country had to be done on horseback along bridle paths, which were frequently so indistinct that the way would be lost. When a traveler reached a stream he rarely found a bridge across it, and he would have to ford it or else swim over, in order to continue his journey. Toward the end of the seventeenth century, some coaches, chaises, and chariots began to be seen; but not till the eighteenth century did even the wealthy use them generally.

Advantages of the Plantation Life. — Though the Virginia social system had its elements of weakness, yet it possessed also its strong points. In it were to be found gallantry, chivalry, and love of honor. It was adorned by the gentler virtues of life, and it developed a broad manliness of character in the people. When the Revolution came, it brought many changes in habits and customs, but disturbed in no radical way plantation life, which preserved its distinctive features till the system went down in the wreck that followed the Civil War.

QUESTIONS

1. In what century was colonial life at its best?
2. Of what classes was society composed?
3. Describe the life on a large plantation.
4. What is said of the life of a planter?
5. Give a description of Mrs. Washington's home life.
6. What is Bishop Meade's comment?
7. Describe the " Great House."
8. What of the architecture of this period?
9. What is said of the overseer's house?
10. Tell of the furniture.
11. Describe the kitchen, and the method of cooking.
12. Tell of the negro quarters.
13. How were the negroes generally treated by their masters?
14. What does Bruce say of this?
15. Describe the planter's dress, and that of his wife.
16. What of the roads, and how was traveling done?
17. What were the advantages of plantation life?

REVIEW QUESTIONS

1. What is said of the governors who ruled after Bacon's Rebellion?
2. When and where was William and Mary College founded?
3. Who was Alexander Spotswood, and when was he appointed governor?
4. Give an account of his crossing the Blue Ridge.
5. When and by whom were the cities of Richmond and Petersburg founded?
6. What caused the French and Indian War?
7. Why did Virginia send a protest to the French commander?
8. Whom did she select to carry her protest, and what is said of his early life?
9. Describe his journey, and its result.
10. How did the hostilities begin?
11. Who was General Braddock, and how was he defeated?
12. Tell of the close of the war, and what possessions were yielded by France to England?
13. What is said of colonial life at its golden age, and of the classes that formed society?
14. Describe the life on a large plantation, the life of the planter, and that of his wife.
15. What is said of the "Great House," and other buildings of this age?
16. Describe the furniture, kitchen, and negro quarters.
17. What is said of the relation of master and servant?
18. Describe the dress of a wealthy planter and that of his wife.
19. Tell of the educational advantages of this period, and how traveling was done.
20. What advantages had plantation life?

CHRONOLOGICAL TABLE OF IMPORTANT EVENTS (1492-1763)

1492. Columbus discovered America.
1497. John Cabot discovered Labrador.
1585. Sir Walter Raleigh's first Roanoke colony.
1587. Sir Walter Raleigh's second Roanoke Island colony.
1606. First charter granted to Virginia.

1607. The English made a settlement at Jamestown; the first permanent English settlement in America, May 13.

1609. Virginia received her second charter.

1610. The Starving Time.

1612. Virginia received her third charter.

1612. Culture of tobacco commenced.

1613. Pocahontas married John Rolfe.

1617. Death of Pocahontas.

1618. The Great Charter issued.

1619. First Colonial Assembly convened at Jamestown, July 30.

1619. Slavery introduced into Virginia.

1622. Indian massacre.

1624. Virginia becomes a royal province. ·

1644. Second Indian massacre.

1649–60. Virginia under the Commonwealth.

1653. Virginians establish a settlement on Albemarle Sound in North
Carolina.

1660. Navigation Acts put into operation.

1673. Culpeper and Arlington grant.

1676. Bacon's Rebellion.

1693 William and Mary College founded.

1732. Washington born, February 22.

1733. Founding of Richmond and Petersburg.

1754. The French and Indian War begun.

1754. Battle of Great Meadows.

1755. Braddock's defeat. ·

1758. Fort Duquesne captured.

1763. End of the French and Indian War

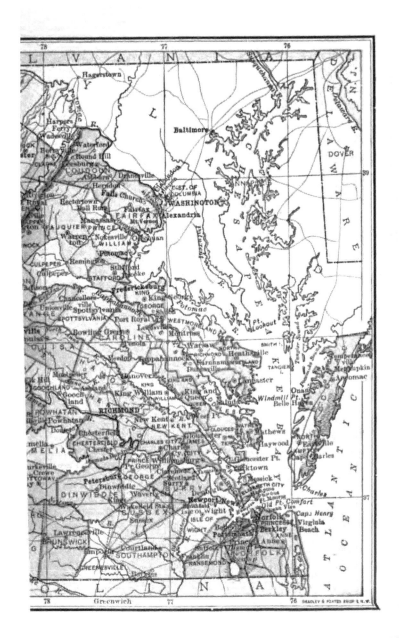

SECOND PERIOD—FROM THE REVOLU-TION TO THE CIVIL WAR

CHAPTER XV

CAUSES THAT LED TO THE REVOLUTION

Condition of the Colony after the War with France. — After the termination of the war between England and France, Virginia enjoyed a period of peace, during which she increased rapidly in population, and was blessed with abundant prosperity. The people, as their country grew and developed began to feel more and more strongly that they were able to take care of themselves, and so they were more disposed than they had ever been, to resist any encroachment upon their rights and privileges. The time soon came when they felt justified in resisting by force of arms even the mother country, to which they had so long acknowledged allegiance.

George III

Opposition to the King's Prerogative. — George III., who ascended the English throne in 1760, was a man of strong convictions, but very narrow and bigoted; and he determined to enjoy all royal prerogatives to the fullest extent, and if possible, to increase them. One of the rights that had been exercised by the king was that of vetoing colonial legislation; but in England he dared not veto an act of Parliament. As time passed, this prerogative of the king began to be called into question more and more; for it was held that acts of the House of Burgesses should be as supreme for Virginia in regard to all local matters, as those of Parliament were for Great Britain.

The Parsons' Case. — The opposition to the veto power of the king, which came out in 1763 in the famous Parsons' Case, gave one of the first indications of an approaching conflict. Briefly stated, the case was as follows:

Patrick Henry

Tobacco was used as money; and the House of Burgesses, at a time when a failure in the crop made the settlement of obligations press heavily upon the people, passed an act that all debts which were to be paid in tobacco could be settled in money, at the rate of twopence per pound for tobacco. The clergymen had been receiving sixpence per pound. They appealed to the king, and he annulled the law. Thereupon Rev. James Maury brought suit in the county court of Hanover to obtain what was due him. When the case, which was regarded as a test one, came up for final trial, Patrick Henry[1] appeared in behalf of the people, and leaving out of consideration the technicalities of the case, boldly denied the right of the king to annul legislation that was for the good of the people, declaring in regard to this particular act of the Burgesses

---

[1] Patrick Henry (1736–1799) was born in Hanover County and first rose to distinction in the Parsons' Case. He was one of Virginia's earliest and most ardent patriots and became America's greatest orator.

that " a king who annulled and disallowed laws of so salutary a nature instead of being the father of his people,
degenerated into a tyrant, and forfeited all right to obedience." His eloquence won the case; for though the jury
was compelled, as the law stood, to decide in favor of the
plaintiff, yet a verdict was returned after a few minutes'
deliberation, awarding one penny damages. The an-
nouncement was received with a shout of applause, and
Henry's friends, in token of their appreciation of his
matchless effort, carried him round the court green upon
their shoulders.

Power of Parliament. — The theory held by the people
as to the allegiance they owed to Great Britain was, that
Virginia constituted an integral part of the king's dominions, subject to the king but not to Parliament. They,
therefore, denied the right of Parliament to legislate for
them in regard to local matters, or to exercise jurisdiction
over the House of Burgesses. While much irritation was
caused when the king annulled acts of the Burgesses, yet
more serious trouble arose when Parliament, under the
influence of George III. and his party, decided to lay a
direct tax upon the people without the consent of the
House of Burgesses, a thing that Charles II. had promised
should not be done.

The Stamp Act. — The first attempt thus to levy taxes
was in 1765, when Parliament passed the Stamp Act,
which required that the colonies should use upon all documents, pamphlets, newspapers, and almanacs, revenue
stamps costing from a half penny up to fifty pounds. As
a result of this law, it was expected that a handsome sum
would be raised annually for the Crown, which would help
Great Britain to pay off the heavy debt she had incurred
in her wars in Europe.

Patrick Henry's Resolutions. — When the Stamp Act came up for discussion in the House of Burgesses, Patrick Henry, who was now a member and a popular leader, offered resolutions declaring that only the House of Burgesses, together with the king or his substitutes, had the right to levy taxes, and that any attempt to take this power

Patrick Henry addressing the House of Burgesses

from the House of Burgesses was unconstitutional. He urged the adoption of these spirited resolutions with an ardor that alarmed the more conservative members of the House. Suddenly, while speaking against the Stamp Act, he exclaimed, "Cæsar had his Brutus, Charles the First his Cromwell, and George the Third" — cries of "Treason! Treason!" here interrupted him. But fixing his eye upon the Speaker of the House, he added, "and George the

Third may profit by their example. If this be treason, make the most of it."

Repeal of the Stamp Act. — The resolutions went through; and the news of what had happened in Virginia was carried with wonderful quickness all over the country. Other colonies adopted similar resolutions, and everywhere such a determined spirit of opposition was manifested to the Stamp Act, that it was found to be impossible to put it into execution, the people absolutely refusing to use the stamps. Finally Parliament yielded, and in 1766 repealed the Stamp Act, but at the same time declared that it had legislative supremacy over the colonies.

A Second Attempt at Taxation. — There was much rejoicing in Virginia when the repeal of the Stamp Act became known, but it was of short duration; for Great Britain had by no means abandoned her plan of taxing the colonies. The year following, Parliament laid duties on tea, paper, glass, and painter's colors. Against this, complaints were heard on all sides; and the loyalty of the people was much weakened by the irritation caused by Great Britain's policy.

The Virginia Resolves. — In 1769, the House of Burgesses passed the famous Virginia resolves, in which they boldly affirmed that the colonies alone had the right to tax themselves, and protested against having persons who were accused of treason carried to England for trial, as Parliament proposed to do on account of the disturbances in America.

The Non-Importation Agreement. — When Lord Botetourt, who was governor at this time, heard what had happened, he felt that, as the king's representative, he could not indorse such rebellious proceedings, and so he at once dissolved the Burgesses; but they met again at the Raleigh

Tavern in Williamsburg, reaffirmed their action, and, in addition, unanimously adopted an agreement not to import commodities from England till the duties were taken off. The Non-Importation Agreement was presented to the Burgesses by George Washington, but it was drawn up by George Mason,[1] who was one of the greatest men of the revolutionary epoch.

George Mason

The Duties repealed except the one on Tea. — The other colonies, animated by the spirited course with which Virginia contended for her rights, passed similar resolutions, and in some cases adopted hers as their own. The Non-Importation Agreement became quite general; and the British government, finding the colonies on the verge of rebellion, repealed all the duties except one of threepence per pound on tea, which was retained for the purpose of establishing a precedent for taxation. The colonies, however, decided that they would purchase no tea till the duty was taken off. Thus for a time matters stood.

Committee of Correspondence. — It became evident, as the dispute with Great Britain continued, that there

[1] George Mason (1726–1792) born in Stafford County. He was a descendant of a member of Parliament who took sides with Charles I., and who emigrated to Virginia after the overthrow of that unfortunate monarch.

must be some way of securing united action. To bring about this desirable object, the House of Burgesses appointed a committee of correspondence, the duty of which was to give the people news of what was taking place in Great Britain, and to keep up communication with the other colonies. Lord Dunmore, who had succeeded Botetourt as governor, on hearing of what had happened, hastily dissolved the Burgesses; but the important action they had taken led to the formation of · similar committees by the thirteen colonies that afterwards constituted the United States. The meaning of this was that henceforth there would be unity of action.

Destruction of the Tea at Boston. — In the other colonies, as well as in Virginia, the people, actuated by a love of freedom, made vigorous resistance to the policy pursued by Great Britain. Massachusetts, though not more determined than Virginia to contend for her rights, had been so open in her opposition that British troops had been quartered in Boston. This led to a collision between the soldiers and the citizens, which inflamed the passions of the people to the highest pitch; and now an event happened which gave them an opportunity to display their defiance of British authority. The East India Company shipped supplies of tea to different American ports to be sold in the colonies. Three vessels brought cargoes to Boston. An organized party, disguised as Indians, boarded the ships, and threw the tea into the sea. When news of these bold proceedings reached England, Parliament ordered that the port of Boston should be closed on the 4th of June 1774, and the city cut off from all trade.

Virginia Fspouses the Cause of Massachusetts. — The House of Burgesses was in session, when the action of the British government against Boston became known in Williamsburg. The consideration of all other business was at once postponed, and a protest was passed against what had been done on the ground that it was subversive of liberty. The 1st of June was appointed a day of fasting, humiliation, and prayer. Again Lord Dunmore dissolved the Burgesses; but the next day they met, regardless of him, at the Raleigh Tavern in Williamsburg, and issued a call for a general congress. Massachusetts had already done the same thing; and the measure met with approbation, all the colonies appointing delegates except Georgia.

The First Congress. — The first Congress met at Philadelphia, on September 5, 1774. Its proceedings were calm and moderate. A declaration of rights was drawn up, and two addresses issued, one to the people of Great Britain, and the other to the people of the colonies. At this time there were but few men who wished the colonies to renounce their allegiance to Great Britain.

The wise action of this representative assembly won many friends in England for the cause of the colonies. " I know not," said Lord Chatham in the House of Lords, "the people or Senate, who, in such a complication of difficult circumstances, can stand in preference to the delegates of America assembled in General Congress in Philadelphia."

QUESTIONS

1. What was the condition of the colony after the war with France?
2. What kind of a man was George III., and what right did he claim
3. How did the people of Virginia regard this?
4. Give an account of the Parsons' Case.
5. Who appeared in behalf of the people, and what were his words?
6. What was the verdict, and what is said of Patrick Henry?

7. What was the theory held by the people as to their allegiance to Great Britain?
8. Hence what right did they deny Parliament?
9. What did George III. now do?
10. What was the Stamp Act, and what was England's object in passing it?
11. Give the resolutions of Patrick Henry.
12. While speaking against the Stamp Act, what did he exclaim?
13. Why was it found impossible to put the Stamp Act into execution?
14. What was Parliament forced to do?
15. The following year a tax was laid on what articles?
16. This led to what action on the part of the Burgesses?
17. When the governor heard this, what did he do, and with what result?
18. What was the Non-Importation Agreement, and by whom drawn up?
19. Did the other colonies follow Virginia's example?
20. What did England agree to do, and how was this received by the colonies?
21. What did the House of Burgesses decide to appoint?
22. What important action did this bring about?
23. What was happening in the other colonies?
24. What became of the tea that was sent to Boston?
25. What order did Parliament give on hearing of this?
26. How did Virginia show her sympathy for Massachusetts?
27. What happened at Raleigh Tavern?
28. When and where did our first Congress meet?
29. What is said of its proceedings?
30. What did Lord Chatham say with regard to its action?

CHAPTER XVI

THE LAST EVENTFUL YEARS OF LORD DUNMORE'S ADMINISTRATION

Lord Dunmore's War. — While the colonies were on the eve of war with Great Britain, Virginia was called upon once more to defend her western frontier from the savages, who rose in arms to drive the settlers out of the territory south of the Ohio River. The struggle which followed was called Dunmore's war, because the governor was charged with having brought it on through his agent, Dr. Conolly, who made statements which the backwoodsmen understood to be equivalent to a declaration of hostilities. The trouble began with the killing of some friendly Shawnees by a party of whites. This unprovoked act was followed by the murder of the entire family of a friendly chief named Logan. These and other outrages committed by the whites, caused a number of western tribes to unite under the leadership of a famous chief called Cornstalk, and begin a war of extermination on the settlers west of the mountains. Lord Dunmore hastily collected an army to meet the impending danger, and proceeded to the seat of war.

Battle of Point Pleasant. — As one wing of Dunmore's army, which was commanded by General Andrew Lewis,[1]

[1] Andrew Lewis (1730–1780), who commanded the Virginians in this decisive encounter, was a native of Ireland. In person, he was more than six feet in height, and possessed great strength and activity; in character he was brave and cautious. He fought under Washington at Great Meadows and was at Braddock's defeat. On the whole, he was just the man to be a border hero.

was about to cross the Ohio River, it was suddenly attacked by the savages in great numbers. A hard-fought battle then took place, which lasted from sunrise till nearly sunset; but in the end the Virginians won a complete victory, though at the loss of a number of brave men. The Indians then made a treaty with Lord Dunmore, promising that they would no more hunt south of the Ohio nor disturb voyagers on the river. This battle was important, because it opened the way for the settlement of Kentucky, and enabled Virginia a few years later to conquer her western territory, and thus make good her title to it.

The Prophetic Words of Patrick Henry. — The Indian war being over, the contest with Great Britain occupied the attention of the public to a greater extent than ever. The situation had now become alarming, and the people began to arm themselves. On the 20th of March, 1775, a convention for the consideration of public affairs met at Richmond in St. John's Church. Patrick Henry promptly introduced a measure for arming and drilling a body of militia; and, in advocating its adoption, he made his famous speech, the closing words of which were: "If we wish to be free, we must fight. It is too late to retire from the contest. There is no retreat but in submission and slavery. The war is inevitable, and let it come. The next gale that sweeps from the North will bring to our ears the clash of resounding arms. I know not what course others will take, but as for me, give me liberty or give me death."

The First Clash of Arms. — His words seemed almost prophetic; for on April 18, 1775, a detachment of British troops was ordered by General Gage, the British commander at Boston, to proceed to Concord and destroy some military stores which the Americans had collected. When the soldiers reached Lexington, they encountered a body

St. John's Church, Richmond

of Massachusetts minutemen, and a collision occurred i
which the first blood of the Revolution was shed. This wa
followed by a second engagement at Concord; and, wit
these skirmishes, the struggle that had so long been in
pending commenced.

The Gunpowder. — The day after the battle of Lexingtoi
Lord Dunmore had a quantity of gunpowder removed froi
the old powder magazine at Williamsburg, and put o
board a British man-of-war lying off Yorktown. Whe
this became known in Williamsburg, the people flew t
arms and were with difficulty restrained from attacking th
governor's palace. In other parts of Virginia also, th
incident caused the greatest excitement. In Frederick
burg, more than six hundred minutemen assembled t
march against the governor; but George Washington an

Edmund Pendleton induced them to disband. This they did after signing a paper in which they pledged themselves to defend "Virginia or any sister colony." The paper closed with the words: "God save the liberties of America," which now took the place of "God save the King." But Patrick Henry thought the time for action had come. He put himself at the head of a Hanover company, and set out for Williamsburg. As he drew near, he was met by a messenger from Lord Dunmore with an offer to pay for the powder, and he accepted this settlement of the matter.

Flight of Lord Dunmore. — About two months later, Lord Dunmore, not deeming it safe for him to remain in Williamsburg longer, took refuge on the *Fowey*, a man-of-war, which

Removing Powder from the Magazine at Williamsburg

was anchored near Yorktown. Before taking his departure, he addressed a communication to the Burgesses, stating that he deemed it advisable for the safety of himself and family to leave Williamsburg. In reply, the Council and the House of Burgesses jointly invited him to return to the head of affairs, assuring him that they would unite in carrying out any plan that might be deemed necessary for his personal safety. But he declined to leave his place of

VIRG. HIST. — *9*

refuge, though he offered to continue to discharge his functions as governor on board the man-of-war. After this, the Burgesses had no further communications with him; and thus the royal government in Virginia came to an end, after it had existed for more than a hundred and fifty years.

Flight of Lord Dunmore

Provisional Government organized. — The Burgesses now saw that it was necessary to provide an executive for Virginia, and so a convention was called, which met in Richmond on July 17, and committed the supreme authority not to one person, but to the famous Committee of Safety.[1] This body was endowed with absolute power, being responsible only to the convention. It was fortunate that this

[1] The "Committee of Safety" consisted of Edmund Pendleton, George Mason, John Page, Richard Bland, Thomas Ludwell Lee, Paul Carrington, Dudley Digges, William Cabell, Carter Braxton, James Mercer, and John Tabb.

provisional government was organized so promptly, for the people had soon to protect themselves from the governor they had renounced.

Dunmore's Ravages. — Lord Dunmore, incensed at his expulsion from his government, decided to make war on Virginia with such forces as he could collect. He had at his command a fleet of several ships and two companies of regulars. With these he commenced a series of predatory incursions along the shores of the Chesapeake. He made his headquarters in Norfolk. From there, he proclaimed martial law and offered freedom to all slaves who would join him and fight against their masters. By such means as these, he collected a mixed force sufficient to enable him to do much damage. But, in December, he was defeated at Great Bridge near Norfolk by a company of Virginians under Colonel William Woodford, and forced to embark on his ships. On the 1st of January, 1776, he bombarded Norfolk, and under cover of the cannonade, a body of marines landed and at his command set fire to the town. After this exploit Dunmore carried on for some months along the shores of the various rivers of eastern Virginia, hostilities that bore more resemblance to the incursions of pirates than to open, honorable war, affording the melancholy spectacle of a governor plundering the people whom he had come to rule over and protect. Finally, he fortified himself at Gwynn's Island at the head of the Piankatank River in Mathews County. From this retreat he was driven by General Andrew Lewis, of Point Pleasant fame, and this was the last of Dunmore in Virginia. He retired first to New York, and then in a short time went back to England, where he entertained royalists who fled from Virginia, and continued to manifest the bitterest hostility to the American cause.

QUESTIONS

1. While the colonies were on the eve of war, what was Vir̩ called to do?
2. How did the trouble begin, and by what was it known?
3. What did the Indians now do?
4. Who was General Andrew Lewis?
5. Tell of the battle of Point Pleasant.
6. What treaty did Lord Dunmore make with the Indians?
7. Why was this battle so important?
8. What contest now occupied the people?
9. When and where was a convention held?
10. What measure was introduced by Patrick Henry?
11. Give his prophetic words.
12. When and where was the first clash of arms?
13. What act of Governor Dunmore's enraged the people?
14. What did they attempt to do?
15. Who induced them to disband?
16. What was the nature of the paper signed?
17. What action did Patrick Henry take, and with what result?
18. Give an account of the flight of Lord Dunmore.
19. What action did the Burgesses take, and with what result?
20. How long had the royal government lasted in Virginia?
21. Tell of the provisional government organized.
22. What did Lord Dunmore now decide to do?
23. Where did he make his headquarters, and what did he proclaiᵢ
24. What occurred at Great Bridge?
25. How and where did he continue his depredations?
26. What was the last of Dunmore in Virginia?

CHAPTER XVII

Operations at the North. — While Virginia was defend-
ing herself from Lord Dunmore, stirring events had
been taking place at the North. The skirmishes at Lexington and Concord were followed a few weeks later by
the capture of Ticonderoga and Crown Point by the
Americans. Generals Howe, Clinton, and Burgoyne came
from England with reinforcements for General Gage,
while an American army of some fifteen thousand collected around Boston and laid siege to the city. The hotly
contested battle of Bunker Hill, which was fought on June
17, 1775, settled the question that there would be a war.
It proved, too, a source of much encouragement to the
Americans; for though they were driven from the field,
they had, by their gallant defense of their position, shown
that they could measure arms with the disciplined troops
of England.

Washington Appointed Commander in Chief. — In view
of the public need, Congress met in Philadelphia and,
after declaring that hostilities had commenced with Great
Britain, appointed George Washington, who was a delegate
from Virginia, commander in chief of the army at Boston.
He accepted the position, but refused to receive any pay
for his services. On his way to his post of duty, he heard
of the battle of Bunker Hill, and at once asked, " Did the

militia stand fire?" Receiving an affirmative answer,
replied, "Then the liberties of the country are safe."

Washington's Appointment a Political Necessity. — W;
ington well deserved the honor of being put at the hea
the army; for he was the only soldier in any of the colo:
of more than a local reputation, the one able leader of 1
who had been tried and found to be competent. At
same time, his appointment was a political necessity. '
Northern colonies recognized the importance of enlis

Virginia actively in the 1
for it was known that all
Southern colonies would fol
her. As she was the m
ancient, the most popul
and the most influential of
colonies, and the devotior
her people to the cause of p
lar liberty commanded res
everywhere, her influence
absolutely necessary to b:
about a union of all the c

Washington

nies into one political b
without which nothing of importance could be acc
plished.

Virginia takes an Active Part in the War. — Now
hostilities had actually commenced, Virginia did not b
tate as to her duty. She threw herself into the strug
with all her strength, and responded promptly to the
of Congress for troops, her quota being fixed at fift
battalions. Volunteers formed themselves into compan
and set out for the seat of war, even while their own ho:
were threatened with destruction by Lord Dunmore. U
every battlefield of the war, Virginia was well represen

She was in her structure and temper more thoroughly English than any of the colonies ; and the soldiers she put in the field were the equals of any Great Britain could bring against them.

First Period of the War. — At first tne war was waged for a redress of grievances, not for separation from Great Britain. The colonies were not ready for the contest; and Washington, who well knew what an army ought to be, occupied himself for some time in drilling and equipping the main army, which he had to do in the face of great difficulties, and while thus engaged he kept up the siege of Boston.

Virginia takes Action for Independence. — Virginia had ever shown herself most jealous of her constitutional rights. In their defense she had, under Bacon, risen in open rebellion in 1676; and now, one hundred years later, she took a step in the cause of freedom which proved to be far-reaching in its effects upon the destinies of America. On May 15, 1776, she, through her convention which met in Williamsburg, instructed her delegates in Congress to propose that the United Colonies should be declared independent. This action was on the next day read to the troops at Williamsburg, and was received by them and by the people generally with loud acclamation.

Bill of Rights. — After instructing the delegates in Congress, the convention on the same day adopted a Bill of Rights which contained a clear exposition of the American theory of government; for it declared the equality of men politically, that they possessed certain inherent rights, such as " the enjoyment of life and liberty, with the means of acquiring and possessing property and pursuing and obtaining happiness and safety," of which they could not by any compact deprive their posterity ; that government

Thomas Jefferson

was derived from the people and was to be used for the benefit of all, and that when not so used the majority had the right to alter or abolish it; that the press should be free, and that men should have the right to follow their consciences in religion.

Adoption of a Constitution. — The Bill of Rights was followed on June 29 by the adoption of a constitution, which made the government consist of a House of Delegates and a Senate, and provided that these should elect annually a governor and a privy council to assist him. This constitution, which was the first written one in the world, contained also a declaration of independence. Thus Virginia proclaimed herself an independent commonwealth amid the universal rejoicing of her people. Her new government went into operation at once, Patrick Henry being elected governor and Edmund Randolph attorney general.

Congress adopts the Declaration of Independence. — When the Virginia delegates in Congress received the instructions from the convention, Richard Henry Lee brought in a motion, "That these United Colonies are and ought to be free and independent

Jefferson's Desk

states, and that all political connections between them and the State of Great Britain is and ought to be dissolved." After a three days' debate the motion was adopted, and a committee was appointed to draw up a Declaration of Independence. The Declaration was written by Thomas Jefferson;[1] and Congress, after making a few changes, adopted it as written by him, on July 4, 1776.

[1] Thomas Jefferson (1743-1826). Next to Washington, Jefferson had more influence in forming the institutions of the country than any of the early

Virginia among the First. — Virginia was first among the foremost in the resolutions condemning the Stamp Act, in the formation of the Committee of Correspondence, in the movement for a Continental Congress, and in the decisive steps that led to the independence of America. More considerate treatment by the British government would have kept her loyal; but, under a sense of oppres-

sion, the revolutionary impulse caused her to renounce utterly an allegiance of which she had in former days been proud to boast.

A Seal Adopted. — After declaring herself independent, Virginia adopted a new seal, devised by George Wythe,[1] which expressed the spirit that animated the people. It represents Virtue, the tutelary goddess of the commonwealth, draped as an Amazon, bearing in one

statesmen. He was the great apostle of popular sovereignty, believing most strongly as he did in the reign of the people and not in that of an aristocracy of birth or of money; he was the real founder of the Democratic party. While universal suffrage was the logical outcome of Jefferson's political doctrines, yet he realized the danger of placing power in the hands of the ignorant, and so we find that the education of the people was one of the objects for which he labored most earnestly. Through his influence the University of Virginia was established in 1819; and he lived long enough to see it go into successful operation. His long life was characterized by the most distinguished services to his native state and to the country at large. He was Secretary of State under Washington, President for two terms, minister to France, governor of Virginia and her representative in Congress.

[1] George Wythe (1726-1806). An eminent lawyer, who was born in Virginia. In 1776, he was a commissioner with Jefferson and others to revise the statutes of Virginia. He was Professor of Law at William and Mary, where he was educated. He was a member of the Virginia Convention, which ratified the Federal Constitution in 1788.

hand a spear and in the other a sword, trampling under foot tyranny, symbolized as a prostrate man, having near him a broken chain and a scourge, while his crown has fallen from his head. Above the figure of Virtue is the word " Virginia," and underneath the motto — " Sic semper tyrannis."

Religious Liberty. — The Episcopal Church had been the established church in Virginia, as it is in England to-day; and at times, harsh laws had been enacted against those who dissented from its doctrines. But one form of belief does not satisfy all people; and at the time of the Revolution, Quakers, Baptists, Presbyterians, and Methodists had gained a strong foothold. In her Bill of Rights, Virginia was the first state in the world to separate absolutely Church and State, declaring as she did that her government should be built upon the foundation stone of religious liberty ; and when the General Assembly met in October, 1776, all persons who did not accept the doctrines of the Established Church were determined to see that laws should be enacted to carry out the principles of religious freedom that had been announced. A great struggle ensued, which lasted for nearly two months. Edmund Pendleton[1] and John Page[2] defended the Episcopal Church, while Thomas Jefferson was the champion

[1] Edmund Pendleton (1721–1803). He was born in Carolina County, Va., was a lawyer by profession, and was known as a conservative statesman. During the Revolution, his object was " to raise the spirits of the timid to a general united opposition," and to oppose the violent who wished to adopt rash measures. He was president of the Committee of Safety, of a number of conventions, and of the Virginia Supreme Court.

[2] John Page (1743–1808). He was born at Rosewell, Va., and was an ardent supporter of the cause of the colonists during the Revolution, contributing of his own private means for the public good. He was a member of the convention that framed the constitution of Virginia, and held a number of other offices. In 1802, he was elected governor of Virginia.

of the dissenters. Religious freedom finally won a complete triumph. Penalties for nonconformity to the rites
of the Episcopal Church were abolished, and all men were
left free to worship God according to the dictates of their
own consciences.

The Law of Primogeniture. — In England, when a man
dies, his property is not distributed equally among his
children, but it goes to his eldest son, and in this way the
aristocracy is kept up. This Law of Primogeniture, as it
is called, had been in full force in Virginia; but now an
attack was made upon it by Thomas Jefferson, who wished,
as he himself stated, to "eradicate every fiber of ancient
and future aristocracy." Edmund Pendleton, who was
the most conservative of the Revolutionary leaders, defended it with great skill; but the bill for its repeal passed
the General Assembly without amendment, and it ceased
to be a law.

A Dictator Proposed. — The first military operations after
the Declaration of Independence were disastrous to the
Americans. In the summer of 1776, General Howe, who
had succeeded General Gage as commander in chief of the
British troops, defeated the American army at Long
Island, in consequence of which Washington was forced
to abandon New York and New Jersey, and retire across
the Delaware into Pennsylvania. To the General Assembly, the outlook seemed so gloomy that it was
proposed to appoint a dictator for Virginia, who should
have absolute power, both civil and military, over persons
and property, the precedent for such action being sought
in the history of Rome. The discussion of this measure
created feelings so bitter that its advocates and its oppo-
nents would not walk on the same side of the street
together. To Patrick Henry, who was to receive the

appointment, Archibald Cary,[1] the leader of the opposition, sent the message that on the day he became dictator, he should fall from a thrust of his dagger.   There is no evidence that Patrick Henry either knew of or approved the scheme.   The plan was suddenly dropped, and it appears to have been but a desperate measure that was considered to meet a desperate need.

Washington crossing the Delaware

Washington restores Confidence. — A few weeks later, Washington restored confidence by recrossing the Delaware, and winning the brilliant victories at Trenton and Princeton.   The people now began to realize his greatness and to esteem him the equal of any commander of antiquity, for he showed that along with a cause full of grandeur, he possessed the genius needed to defend it.

[1] Archibald Cary (1730-1786). He was born in Virginia, and was a relative of Lord Falkland. He was a conspicuous patriot in the Revolution, his services being mainly in the Virginia Convention and in the House of Burgesses. When the state government was organized, he was elected President of the Senate.

Burgoyne's Invasion. — The next summer General Burgoyne left Canada with a part of the British army and marched by way of Lake Champlain into New York, his plan being to seize the line of the Hudson and cut New England off from the Middle and Southern states. All went well with him till he reached the upper Hudson, where the American army under General Gates had taken a stand to oppose his further progress. Burgoyne had in his army a number of Indians; and these ferocious allies so harassed the Americans that Gates wrote Washington that they almost produced a panic.

Daniel Morgan

Morgan and his Riflemen. — Washington had among his troops a corps of picked Virginia riflemen from the Shenandoah valley and the upper James, commanded by the distinguished Colonel Daniel Morgan. These he sent to reinforce Gates. It is said that the aim of these men was so accurate "that any one of them could toss up an apple and shoot all the seeds out of it as it fell." Accustomed to the Indian method of warfare, they soon struck terror into the breasts of the savages, who said that the rifles of these sharpshooters "were more terrible than the lightnings of the Great Spirit." They certainly contributed much to turn the tide of battle against Burgoyne. At Bemis Heights, near Saratoga, where Burgoyne fought a desperate battle in an unsuccessful attempt to drive the Americans from their position, the Virginia riflemen dispersed the Canadians and Indians, who covered the flanks of the right wing of Burgoyne's army and were brought to a stand only when they encountered the British line of battle. A few weeks later, when Burgoyne made a reconnaissance with fifteen hundred picked men, drawn up in three columns, Morgan's corps fell upon the right column, which was commanded by General Frasier, and

Burgoyne's Surrender

forced it to fall back, Frasier himself being mortally wounded by one of the riflemen.

Burgoyne's Surrender. — After these reverses Burgoyne retired to Saratoga, where, on October 17, 1777, he surrendered his entire army to General Gates. The political effect of this victory in Europe was very great. France had favored the Americans from the first, and had rendered them some aid. This she had done secretly; but, after the surrender of Burgoyne, she acknowledged the independence of the thirteen United Colonies and on February 6, 1778, entered into a treaty, promising to help them with money, men, and war supplies. Saratoga is put down by Sir Edward Creasy as one of the fifteen decisive battles of the world; and much of the credit of winning it justly belongs to the Virginians.

QUESTIONS

1. What events were occurring in the North?
2. What battle had decided the question of war, when and where fought?
3. Who was chosen commander, and on what condition did he accept?
4. What is said of Washington, and why was his appointment a political necessity?
5. Tell what active part Virginia took in the war, and what of her soldiers?
6. Was the war waged at first for separation from Great Britain?
7. What was Virginia's action for independence?
8. What was the Bill of Rights, and what followed its adoption?
9. What was the Constitution, and what did it contain?
10. Who was elected first governor under this Constitution?
11. What motion did Richard Henry Lee bring up in Congress?
12. Who wrote the Declaration of Independence?
13. Who was Thomas Jefferson?
14. Virginia was foremost in what decisive steps?
15. Describe Virginia's new seal. By whom was it devised?
16. Give the controversy as to religious liberty in Virginia.
17. Who defended the established church, and who the dissenters?
18. What was the result?
19. What was the Law of Primogeniture?
20. Who made an attack upon it, and with what result?
21. Why was a dictator proposed for Virginia?
22. What feelings did this arouse?
23. How did Washington restore confidence?
24. Tell of Burgoyne's invasion.
25. What is said of his Indian allies?

26. Give an account of Morgan and his riflemen.
27. Where was a desperate battle fought, and with what result?
28. When and where did Burgoyne surrender?
29. What did France do after the surrender of Burgoyne?
30. What does Sir Edward Creasy say of the battle of Saratoga?

REVIEW QUESTIONS

1. Why did the colonists object to the veto power of the king?
2. Relate the Parsons' Case.
3. What was the Stamp Act, and why was it repealed?
4. What was the Non-Importation Agreement, and why was it adopted?
5. Why was the tea destroyed at Boston?
6. When and where did the first Congress meet?
7. Give an account of Lord Dunmore's war.
8. When and where was the first clash of arms that marked the beginning of the Revolution?
9. How did the royal government come to end?
10. Describe Dunmore's ravages.
11. What battle settled the question as to war?
12. Who was appointed commander in chief of the colonial troops, and why was his appointment a political necessity?
13. What was the object of the colonists at first, and what active part did Virginia take in the war?
14. Tell of Virginia's action for independence, of her Bill of Rights, and her Constitution.
15. What was the Declaration of Independence, by whom written, and when adopted?
16. In what ways did Virginia take the lead for independence?
17. Describe the seal adopted.
18. Give an account of the controversy for religious liberty.
19. What was the Law of Primogeniture, and through whose influence was it abolished?
20. Why was a dictator proposed, and with what result?
21. Give an account of Burgoyne's invasion.
22. What is said of Morgan and his riflemen?
23. When and where did Burgoyne surrender, and what is said of it?

VIRG. HIST. — 10

CHAPTER XVIII

THE LAST YEARS OF THE REVOLUTION

The War in the South. — After the battle of Saratoga, the British transferred the war from the North to the South. They reduced Georgia and South Carolina to submission; and then Lord Cornwallis, one of their ablest generals, undertook the conquest of North Carolina. The need of troops in the South was so great that Virginia exerted herself to the utmost in gathering recruits and in hurrying them off to the seat of war.

The British attack Virginia. — During the first years of the war, the central position of Virginia had protected her from invasion; but the British now decided to attack her in earnest to keep her from sending so much aid to the South. A fleet was first sent under General Matthews, who took possession of Portsmouth, burned Suffolk, and destroyed at Norfolk and Gosport great quantities of military stores. The British soldiers also made incursions into the country, carrying destruction far and wide, while British men-of-war ruined the coasting trade of the state by destroying more than one hundred ships.

Benedict Arnold in Virginia. — The British followed their first attack by a determined effort to subjugate Virginia, believing that, if she was conquered, this would ensure the permanent subjugation of the Southern states. Early in January, 1781, Benedict Arnold, who a few months before had turned traitor to the American cause, sailed up the

James with an army of nine hundred men, and the invasion began in earnest. Thomas Jefferson, who had succeeded Patrick Henry as governor, called out the militia to defend Richmond. But Baron Steuben, who had general command of military matters in Virginia, had just sent all the men he could raise to the South. Arnold accordingly captured Richmond without opposition. He held possession of the city for a few days, destroyed her archives, plundered her stores, and then returned to Portsmouth, ravaging the country on his way.

Marquis de Lafayette

Lafayette. — In the spring, the British sent General Phillips with two thousand additional troops to Virginia. He captured Petersburg after a skirmish with a body of militia under Steuben, and then proceeded to Richmond. But here he found a body of regular troops drawn up ready to give him battle. They were under the command of the Marquis de Lafayette, an ardent young French nobleman who had come to serve in the American army as a volunteer and without pay; but Congress had commissioned him a major general, and Washington, whose confidence he had won, had sent him to coöperate with Steuben in the defense of Virginia. General Phillips decided not to attack Lafayette, but retreated to Petersburg, where he died from fever a few days after his arrival.

The Virginians at King's Mountain. — While these events had been occurring in Virginia, the war had been prosecuted energetically further South. In conducting the campaign in North Carolina, Cornwallis sent Colonel Ferguson, one of his ablest partisan leaders, with a force of eleven hundred to invade the mountain region. This caused the pioneers of Virginia, Tennessee, and the Carolinas to rise

Battle of King's Mountain

in arms, and soon fourteen hundred assembled, four hundred coming from Washington County, Virginia, under the command of Colonel William Campbell, who was chosen leader of the entire force. Ferguson, finding that he was in danger, retreated to King's Mountain, upon the top of which he took what he regarded as an impregnable position. But the frontiersmen took his camp by storm and all his followers were either killed or captured, he himself being among the slain.

Morgan at Cowpens. — Daniel Morgan and his men were always to be found where fighting was going on, and they were now in the South, where they proved so troublesome to the British that Cornwallis sent Colonel Tarleton with eleven hundred men against them. Tarleton pursued Morgan and coming up with him at Cowpens, a grazing ground not far from King's Mountain, at once attacked him. But Morgan displayed wonderful skill in the way he managed the battle. In an open field he surrounded and nearly annihilated the British forces, which were superior to his own, Tarleton escaping with only two hundred men.

Virginia becomes the Seat of War. — Cornwallis's army was much depleted by the battles he had fought, and so he decided to march northward, unite his forces with the British troops in Virginia, and complete the subjugation of the Old Dominion before he undertook any further operations in the Carolinas. Acting upon this resolution, he reached Petersburg soon after the death of General Phillips, and at once took command of the British troops in Virginia.

Maneuvers of Cornwallis and Lafayette. — Lafayette was at this time below Richmond with about four thousand men, and Cornwallis, with nearly double that number, looked forward to an easy victory over him. " The boy cannot escape me," he wrote in a letter to England. But Lafayette though young had prudence, and was unwilling to risk a battle till he was reinforced by General Wayne, who was coming with eight hundred Pennsylvanians to join him. So as Cornwallis advanced, Lafayette retired till he reached Culpeper County, where he met Wayne. Cornwallis followed as far as Hanover County, where he halted, camping on the North Anna River. While these maneuvers were going on, his cavalry under

Tarleton was laying waste the whole James River country with fire and sword, destroying what they did not need. They made a raid on Charlottesville, hoping to capture the legislature, which was in session in that place, and also Governor Jefferson, who was at Monticello, but failed in this attempt.

Cornwallis Entrapped. — Cornwallis finally selected York-town as the basis of his operations, where he fortified him-self strongly. Washington, learning through Lafayette that the Count de Grasse was coming with a French fleet to take part against the British, at once decided to combine the French and American armies, and capture Cornwallis before he could be reinforced. The plan was kept a secret, the movement being covered under an apparent design of laying siege to New York. This deceived the British till it was too late to relieve Cornwallis, who did not realize his danger till the French fleet appeared in the waters of the Chesapeake, and landed three thousand troops to reinforce Lafayette, followed a few days later by the arrival of Washington and the Count de Rocham-beau with land forces. The combined French and Ameri-can armies amounted to sixteen thousand, and the British army numbered eight thousand. Cornwallis now saw that he was hemmed in both by land and by sea; but he pre-pared to make a desperate defense.

Siege of Yorktown. — The siege of Yorktown now began. For more than a week a vigorous cannonade was kept up and then the outer lines of Cornwallis's works were carried at the point of the bayonet. The British still held the inner fortifications; but these were swept by the fire of the American batteries. The situation of Cornwallis be-coming desperate, on the 19th of October, 1781, he sur-rendered. On this memorable occasion, the Americ

Surrender of Cornwallis

and French troops were drawn up in two columns, Washington and Rochambeau being at their head; and between them the conquered British marched out and laid down their arms, the bands playing "The world's upside down."

Peace at Last. — A great victory had been won; and Congress set apart a day for thanksgiving and prayer, while Washington ordered that all persons under arrest should be set free so that they, too, might share in the general rejoicing. The surrender at Yorktown was virtually the closing scene of the war, and it was fitting that it should occur in the Old Dominion, where the prelude to the Revolution had taken place.

Governor Nelson. — Among the Virginia patriots of the Revolution, Thomas Nelson, who succeeded Jefferson as governor, stands preëminent. He was a man of great wealth, all of which he sacrificed to his country's needs. When two Virginia regiments were ordered to the Carolinas, before the soldiers started, he gave them all that was due them as back pay out of his own private fortune. At a time when the public credit was in a very depressed condition, the state tried to borrow two million dollars to aid

Nelson at the Siege of Yorktown

in carrying on the war, but the amount could not be obtained on the security of the commonwealth. Seeing this, Nelson added his personal security to that of the state, and in this way a large proportion of the sum was raised. At the siege of Yorktown, Nelson noticed that the American gunners refrained from firing at his house which had become a refuge for the British. Thereupon he directed the first gun at it himself, and offered fi——

guineas to the cannoneer who would put the first ball through it. He was for some time before the end of the war commander in chief of the Virginia forces; and Washington made special mention of the services rendered by him in bringing the siege of Yorktown to a successful issue. Nelson has many honorable descendants living in Virginia.

QUESTIONS

1. After the battle of Saratoga, where was the seat of war transferred?
2. Why did the British decide to attack Virginia?
3. What did they do in Portsmouth and elsewhere?
4. In subjugating Virginia, what did they believe would follow?
5. What depredations did Benedict Arnold commit?
6. What did the British do in the spring?
7. Who was Marquis de Lafayette?
8. How had the war progressed in the Carolinas?
9. What was the result of the battle of King's Mountain?
10. Describe the battle of Cowpens.
11. What was Cornwallis's plan after these battles?
12. Give an account of the maneuvers of Cornwallis and Lafayette.
13. Why did Tarleton make a raid on Charlottesville?
14. How did Washington entrap Cornwallis?
15. Describe the siege of Yorktown.
16. When and where did Cornwallis surrender?
17. Describe the situation of the armies at the time.
18. What did Congress order to be done?
19. What is said of the surrender of Cornwallis?
20. Who was Thomas Nelson?
21. In what ways did he show his patriotism?

CHAPTER XIX

British Occupation of the Northwest Territory. — The vast domain north of the Ohio River, Virginia claimed belonged to her by the terms of the charter of 1609, in which her territory was said to reach "up into the land from sea to sea." But the British had taken possession of this country, and had captured from the French the military forts at Kaskaskia and Vincennes. Still, in sentiment, the people were anti-English, and were ready to acknowledge the authority of Virginia.

The "Hannibal of the West." — Before the Revolution ended this territory was brought under the jurisdiction of the Old Dominion, as the result of a most daring enterprise, which was successfully carried through by a native Virginian, George Rogers Clark, whose exploits gave him the title of the "Hannibal of the West." He had moved to Kentucky, which had been made a county of Virginia, and, finding that the Ohio Indians, instigated as he believed by the British, were invading the country, he conceived the daring project of protecting it by conquering the Northwest Territory for Virginia. So he journeyed back to Virginia, and unfolded his plan to Governor Henry, who enthusiastically indorsed the scheme and took steps to equip an expedition to carry it out. Clark was commissioned colonel, supplied with money, and authorized to enlist men in any county of the commonwealth till he had raised seven companies of fifty each. After much difficulty he equipped three companies, and with these he started; but on his way he was joined by some Kentuckians, which raised his force to nearly two hundred.

Capture of Kaskaskia, Cahokia, and Vincennes. — After a long march through the wilderness, he reached Kaskaskia, and attacked the place by night. He thus describes the result. "I immediately divided my little army into two divisions; ordered one to surround the town; with the other, I broke into the fort, secured the governor, Mr. Rocheblave, in fifteen minutes had every street secured; sent runners through the town, ordering the people on pain of death to keep close to their homes, which they observed; and before daylight, had the whole town disarmed." The people, after being assured by Colonel Clark that their rights would be respected, readily took an oath of allegiance to Virginia. They even organized a company of volunteers, who marched to Cahokia, a French town sixty miles north of Kaskaskia, and this settlement gave in its submission. Vincennes, having grown weary of British rule, now surrendered without a struggle, the inhabitants agreeing to garrison the fort, which Clark left in charge of one of his men.

Clark gets Control over the Indians. — The Indians were amazed at what had happened, and their chiefs, within a circuit of five hundred miles, hastened to Cahokia to see the big warrior of the "Long Knives," as they called the Virginians. Clark met them in council, and, showing them a peace belt and a war belt, bade them take their choice, manifesting at the same time no concern as to which they might select. One after another declared for peace; and thus Clark obtained control over them.

Clark at the Indian Council

The British recapture Vincennes. — Clark made this conquest in 1778; but toward the end of the year, Colonel
Hamilton, governor of Canada, descended the Wabash
River with eight hundred men, and recaptured Vincennes.
After this he made preparations for a grand campaign
when the spring opened, his plan being to take Kaskaskia
from Clark, subdue Kentucky, and then, coming further
into Virginia, overrun the settlements west of the Alle-
ghanies. This alarming news Clark obtained from Colonel
Vigo, a Spanish merchant of St. Louis, who also informed
him that for the winter Hamilton had with him at Vincennes
only eighty men to garrison the place, having sent his other
troops away until he should need them in the spring.

Clark surprises Hamilton. — Clark decided, as he himself stated, that he would take Hamilton before Hamilton

could take him, and so he at once set out for Vincennes with his little army. In midwinter he made a march of two hundred and fifty miles, which for hardship has rarely been paralleled. The rivers were swollen by the winter rains, and the Illinois prairies were full of water and ice. For miles in the low grounds of the Wabash River, the troops were compelled to wade through water breast high; but under the influence of their intrepid leader, they persevered in spite of all obstacles. Great was Governor Hamilton's surprise when Clark appeared and demanded his surrender. He made the best defense he could, but finally was forced to submit. Clark sent him to Virginia, a prisoner of war.

Civil Government Organized. — As soon as Virginia had established her claim to her Northwest Territory, Governor Henry appointed Colonel John Todd to administer the civil government. Courts of justice and military companies were organized at Kaskaskia, Cahokia, and Vincennes; and the machinery of a complete civil government set into operation.

Importance of the Conquest. — For the conquest of the country north of the Ohio, Congress never furnished a dollar nor a soldier. The glory of the undertaking belongs exclusively to Colonel Clark and to Virginia. Its importance can hardly be overestimated; for the fact that Virginia was in possession of the country at the close of the Revolution enabled the United States to hold it when peace was made with England. Had it not been conquered by Virginia, it would doubtless be Canadian territory to-day.

QUESTIONS

1. What was the extent of Virginia's Northwest Territory?
2. Who took possession of this territory?
3. What was the sentiment of its people?
4. By whom was it restored to Virginia, and by what title was he known?
5. Who was George Rogers Clark, and what was his plan?
6. Give an account of the capture of the three forts.
7. What did the inhabitants agree to do?
8. How did Clark get control over the Indians?
9. What happened soon after he made this conquest?
10. How did Clark surprise Governor Hamilton?
11. What was the result?
12. What did Virginia do as soon as her claim was established?
13. To whom does the glory of this conquest belong, and why was it such an important one?

CHAPTER XX

VIRGINIA IN THE UNION

Virginia Cedes her Northwest Territory. — The colonies had won their independence by united action; but at the close of the Revolution many rivalries existed between them. The claims which seven of the thirteen states made to western lands, caused so many disputes that the Articles of Confederation, adopted by Congress during the Revolution, were not signed by all the states till 1781. Maryland would not agree to them unless the states owning western land would cede it to the United States. Virginia, earnestly desiring union, surrendered her territory[1] north of the Ohio to bring this about. Her patriotism in this act becomes conspicuous when the greatness of her possessions is considered and the soundness of her title, which was based both upon her charter and upon conquest.

Boundary Dispute between Virginia and Pennsylvania. — The territory beyond the western boundary of Maryland was claimed by both Virginia and Pennsylvania; and in

[1] Virginia gave her Northwest Territory to the United States on condition " that the necessary and reasonable expenses incurred by this state in subduing any British posts or maintaining forts or garrisons within and for the defense, or in acquiring any part of the territory so ceded or relinquished, shall be fully reimbursed by the United States." In speaking of this stipulation, William L. Royall says, "The United States government accepted her (Virginia's) grant upon the express understanding that it would repay her these expenses, which it has never done. With their accumulated interest these expenses would be a very large sum now." — *Virginia State Debt Controversy*, p. 111.

their contest over the matter, they almost went to war. But commissioners, appointed by the states to settle the quarrel, agreed to begin at the Delaware River and to extend Mason and Dixon's line[1] due west five degrees of longitude for the southern boundary of Pennsylvania, and then to draw a meridian from the western extremity of the state to its northern limit for its western boundary. The "Pan-Handle" is the part of Virginia that was left north of Mason and Dixon's line and east of the Ohio River. The extension of the line was not completed till 1785.

Virginia Leads the Movement for a more Perfect Union. —After the Articles of Confederation had been signed they proved insufficient for the government of the country. The states soon began to quarrel in regard to commerce, and some laid taxes on articles imported from others. So great were the difficulties which confronted the Confederation that the legislature of Virginia invited the states to hold a convention to consider the regulation of the trade and commerce of the United States. This convention met in Annapolis in 1786; but, as only five states were represented, the delegates adjourned after passing a resolution requesting the states to call a convention in order to revise the Articles of Confederation. This body met in Philadelphia, and after a discussion which lasted for four months, on September 17, 1787, adopted the present Constitution of the United States.

---

[1] The boundary line between Maryland and Pennsylvania was laid out by two eminent English surveyors, Charles Mason and Jeremiah Dixon, and named after them Mason and Dixon's line. They commenced the line in 1763, but did not finish it till 1767, the delay being chiefly due to Indian troubles. Mason and Dixon's line became the most famous in the United States because it was popularly supposed to separate the slave states from the free states; but this was an error, as Delaware, which is both north and east of the line, was a slave state.

The Constitution Ratified. — There was great opposition to the Constitution in Virginia; and in every county speeches were made for it and against it. The people were divided into two great parties, and much bitterness was manifested in the discussions that took place. On June 2, 1788, a convention met at Richmond, which was now the capital, to consider the adoption of the new plan of government. A vehement struggle occurred, as is shown by the reports of the speeches that were made on this occasion. Patrick Henry led the opposition, and James Madison the party in favor of ratification. Finally on June 25, the Constitution was adopted by a vote of eighty-nine to seventy-nine. The result was largely due to the influence of Washington, which was exerted in favor of the Constitution. It was ultimately signed by all the states.

Virginia Proposes another Revision. — Though Virginia had adopted the Constitution, yet she was far from being satisfied with it. So strong was her belief that some essential changes should be made in it that, in 1788, her legislature addressed a communication to Congress, asking that a new convention should be called to revise it. Fortunately for the permanence of the Union this was not done; but Congress at its first session adopted a number of amendments to the Constitution, which did much to remove the discontent. Notwithstanding this, Virginia was for a long time prominent in her dissatisfaction with the Constitution, her people fearing that under it a strong central government would be formed which would impair the sovereignty of the states.

The Alien and Sedition Laws. — In 1798, during the administration of President Adams, who succeeded Washington, Congress passed the Alien and Sedition Laws, the first giving the President power to banish any foreigner who was regarded as dangerous to the peace of the country, while the second laid heavy penalties upon persons who should resist government officials in the discharge of lawful acts, and upon those who might speak or publish anything that would bring the government or its officers into bad repute. These laws met with a most vigorous oppo-

Mt. Vernon, Washington's Home

sition in Virginia, on the ground that they were an exercise of powers not granted in the Constitution. On December 2, 1798, the legislature passed resolutions, in which it was affirmed that the powers of the government were limited to such as were specially mentioned in the compact between the states, and that, if the Federal government should go beyond the authority given to it, the states had a right to declare such action unconstitutional. The excitement that had been aroused by the obnoxious laws led to no serious result at the time; but the strict interpretation of the Constitution, as expressed in the famous resolutions of 1798, became the fundamental principle of the State-Rights party in Virginia.

Washington's Tomb

The Great Virginian. — Washington was the first President elected under the Constitution. He took the oath of office in New York on April 30, 1789. Of all the great men of Virginia and of the United States, he stands first for ability and distinguished service. His management of the American army during the Revolution places him high in the rank of the world's greatest commanders;

and the wisdom he displayed during his presidency, in carrying the country safely through the dangers tha threatened to subvert it after independence had beer won, gave him a reputation for statesmanship of the high est order.   Truly he was " first in war, first in peace, anc first in the hearts of his countrymen."   He died at hi: home, Mount Vernon, in 1799, beloved by all.

Period of Prosperity. — At the end of the Revolution the people of Virginia were very poor.   The war had taxec their resources to the utmost, and during its last years mucl of their property had been destroyed by the British soldiers But in a few years, a great change for the better set in ; anc toward the close of the eighteenth century, Virginia enterec upon an era of prosperity which extended through more than half of the nineteenth century.   Her tobacco founc ready sale in Europe at high prices, and was the source oi much wealth.   So the people lived in plenty and content ment.   Under the influence of liberal laws, labor had its due reward; and but few paupers were to be found in the state

" The Mother of States and of Statesmen." — A few years after the Revolution, Kentucky, which was a part oi Virginia, was admitted into the Union as a separate state This was done with the consent of Virginia, whose limit: were thus reduced to what is now contained in the tw Virginias.   At a later period, out of the magnificent terr tory north of the Ohio, which Virginia had given to th United States, the great states of Ohio, Indiana, Michiga⁻ Illinois, Wisconsin, and part of Minnesota were succe sively carved ; and thus the Old Dominion became know as the "Mother of States."   She was also called tℑ " Mother of Statesmen," because so many distinguishe men were nurtured on her soil.   She furnished four of the first five presidents — Washington, Jefferson, Madison, and

Monroe, each of whom served two terms. Tyler was also from Virginia, and Harrison, Taylor, and Woodrow Wilson were born in Virginia, though they were residents of other states when elected. Thus she has given to the Union more presidents than any other state.

Burning of the Richmond Theater

Burning of the Richmond Theater. — A domestic calamity that occurred on the night of December 26, 1811, claims a place in history. This was the burning of the Richmond theater, when it was filled with a fashionable audience of about six hundred, who had assembled to witness a drama

called the *Bleeding Nun*. During the performance a
spark fell on the curtain of the stage, and from this the
building was speedily enveloped in flames. A panic ensued, and seventy persons lost their lives, many of whom
belonged to the most influential families in the state.
This memorable disaster filled the city with mourning.
Throughout the state, and indeed all over the country, it
caused the deepest sorrow. The Assembly of Virginia
by resolution requested its members to wear crape for
thirty days, and the same action was taken by Congress.
The next year, Monumental Church was erected where the
theater had been. The church still stands, and at the door
there is a marble monument, upon which are the names of
a number of those who perished in this disaster.

War of 1812.[1] — In the war which the United States
waged against Great Britain in 1812, volunteers enlisted
from all parts of Virginia in the service of their country;
and the state patriotically sustained the Federal government. Only once during the war was the territory of Virginia invaded. This was just a few months before the
termination of hostilities, when Admiral Cockburn, who
commanded a British fleet, entered the waters of the Chesapeake and laid waste its banks. He captured Hampton;

[1] The cause of this war, briefly stated, was as follows: During the first
years of the nineteenth century, England and France were at war, and each
of these nations prohibited American ships from trading with the other. This
nearly ruined the commerce of the United States, and brought on a quarrel
with England. The feeling of hostility toward England, caused by the damage to trade, was further increased by a right she claimed of searching American vessels, and of taking from them English seamen, in order to force them
into her navy. In exercising this right, she did not always stop with her own
subjects, but compelled many American seamen to enter her service. Finally,
the people decided that these outrages could be borne no longer; and, on June
18, 1812, the United States declared war against England. "Free trade and
Sailors' Rights" was the popular cry that brought on the war.

and, during the short time he occupied the place, rendered himself infamous by allowing his soldiers and negroes that followed them to commit outrages of every kind upon the defenseless inhabitants.

What Virginians did for the Union. — During the first half of the nineteenth century, the territory of the United States was nearly quadrupled ; and Virginians were instrumental either directly or indirectly in bringing about the greater part of this tremendous increase of area. The territory of Louisiana was purchased by Thomas Jefferson while he was President. This province, which had been ceded by Spain to France, extended from the Gulf of Mexico on the south to Canada on the north, and from the Mississippi River on the east to the Rocky Mountains on the west ; in securing this, Jefferson more than doubled the area of the United States. Nor was this all that he did to extend the dominion of the Union. In 1804 he sent Captains Lewis and Clark of Albemarle County, Virginia, with a party of men to explore the territory of Louisiana. They ascended the Missouri River as far as they could in boats, and proceeded on foot till they came to its source. After this, making their way across the Rocky Mountains, they explored the valley of the Columbia River, till they reached the Pacific Ocean. The discoveries which were made by Lewis and Clark proved to be important, as they aided the United States, at a later period, in establishing her title to Oregon. President Monroe, during his administration, purchased Florida from Spain, thus adding another large area to the public domain. General Sam Houston, a native of Rockbridge County, led the Texans to victory in their struggle for independence from Mexico. President Tyler, just before the end of his term, signed the resolution passed by Congress for the annexation of Texas.

In the war with Mexico which followed, two Virginians, Generals Taylor and Scott, led the United States armies to victory. Mexico was badly defeated, and had to submit to a dismemberment of her territory, a large part of which came to the United States.[1]

" The Pathfinder of the Sea." — To the scientific investigations of a Virginian, Matthew Fontaine Maury, not only the United States but the whole civilized world is indebted. He entered the navy in 1825, and in 1842 was appointed Superintendent of the Depot of Charts and Instruments at Washington. At this time the sailing maps in use were very inaccurate, and but meager information had been obtained in regard to ocean currents. Maury soon published a chart, which he called a "Fair Way to Rio." This proved to be so accurate and valuable that Congress authorized him to make systematic observations of winds and currents. This he did, and as a result originated a system of "Wind and Current Charts," which was speedily adopted by mariners of all nations. By its use thousands of lives were annually saved and millions of dollars in the cost of voyages. Maury also instituted deep sea soundings,[2] which convinced him that the bottom of the ocean between Newfoundland and Ireland was a plateau, the surface of which was not disturbed by either

[1] This war broke out in 1846, as a result of a dispute between the United States and Mexico in regard to the western boundary of Texas. Mexico was defeated, and in 1848 signed a treaty by which she ceded to the United States all the territory claimed by Texas, and in addition the territory of California and New Mexico, out of which a number of states were made. Many Virginians fought in Mexico, and received there the training which rendered them so efficient as soldiers in 1861, when Virginia felt under the painful necessity of drawing the sword against the Union.

[2] Colonel John M. Brooke of Virginia rendered Maury valuable aid in deep sea soundings by inventing an apparatus which brought up specimens from the bottom of the ocean.

waves or currents. He suggested that the wires of a submarine telegraph could be safely laid upon this. His idea was followed up, and in 1858 Europe and America were connected by the first Atlantic cable. Upon Maury the principal nations of Europe conferred many honors in recognition of his services to mankind. His *Physical Geography of the Sea*, which has been translated into many languages, is an enduring monument to his genius.

Virginia's Influence upon other States. — The Old Dominion, whose hardy pioneers began at an early period to push their way out into the South and West, has done her full part in bringing about the settlement and development of the United States. As early as 1653, ten years before the profligate Charles II. granted North Carolina to "lord proprietors," Roger Greene, with one hundred men from Virginia, settled on the northern shore of Albemarle Sound, and thus laid the foundation of the colony that grew into North Carolina. In 1750, Dr. Thomas Walker and a company of Virginians explored a part of Tennessee and discovered the Cumberland River and Mountains, which they named after the Duke of Cumberland. John Sevier and James Robertson, both Virginians by birth, were the leaders in founding the earliest settlements in Tennessee, and Sevier was elected first governor of the state. In such enterprises as these Virginia has borne a prominent part. Her influence has been great in some states of the West, and the beginning of nearly all government in the South can be traced to her. Her University, which was founded by Thomas Jefferson in 1819, and may justly be called the noblest work of his life, was for a long time the educational center of the whole South. Its halls are still filled with students from many states, and its alumni are to be found all over the country.

QUESTIONS

1. Why did Virginia cede her Northwest Territory to the Union?
2. What is said of her patriotism in this act?
3. Give an account of the disputed boundary line between Virgir and Pennsylvania.
4. What was Mason and Dixon's line?
5. Why did Virginia invite the states to hold a convention?
6. What resolution did this convention pass?
7. When and where did a second convention meet to revise t Articles of Confederation, and what was done?
8. How was the Constitution regarded in Virginia?
9. When did she ratify it?
10. Why did she propose another revision?
11. What were the Alien and Sedition Laws, and why did Virgir oppose them?
12. What resolutions did the legislature adopt in 1798?
13. What is said of George Washington?
14. What is said of Virginia's prosperity?
15. Why was Virginia called the " Mother of States "?
16. Why the " Mother of Statesmen "?
17. Give an account of the burning of Richmond theater.
18. What action was taken by the legislature and Congress in rega to it?
19. What has been erected on the spot?
20. What was the War of 1812?
21. How did Virginia suffer in this war?
22. How much did the territory of the United States increase duri the first half of the nineteenth century?
23. What purchase did Jefferson make while President?
24. Describe the Lewis and Clark expedition.
25. What territory did President Monroe purchase from Spain?
26. Who led the Texans in their war for independence?
27. State the cause of the Mexican War.
28. What part did Virginians take in this war?
29. Who was Matthew Fontaine Maury?
30. How did he benefit mankind?
31. What is said of Virginia's influence upon other states?

CHAPTER XXI

SLAVERY

Encouraged by England. — After the first negroes were brought to Virginia in 1619, so profitable did the slave trade become that England encouraged it in every way. There was at this time no moral sentiment against slavery, as is shown by the fact that Queen Anne herself owned a large part of the stock of the Royal African Company.

Attitude of Virginia. — While the Virginians could use negroes with profit in agriculture, yet the wisdom of making this system of labor the corner stone of the prosperity of the people was early called into question, some of the wisest men foreseeing that it was likely to prove the cause of much disaster. During colonial days over a hundred petitions were sent from Virginia to the king and to Parliament, asking that the further importation of negroes from Africa should be stopped; but these proved unavailing. After the Revolution the feeling against the slave trade continued; and in 1787, when Congress passed the Ordinance for the government of the Northwest Territory, one clause of which prohibited slavery, Virginia fully approved this action. Many of her ablest statesmen regarded the system as a bad one, and hoped the time would come when she herself would be free from it.

New England's Connection with Slavery. — When the Revolution began, slavery existed in all the colonies; but in the North it was dying out, because it was not profitable.

For some time before the Revolution, the people of New England began to engage in the business of importing negroes from Africa to sell to the people of the South, and this soon became to them a money-making employment. So during the Revolution, when a bill, which was favored by Virginia and other states, was brought before Congress to put an end to the slave trade, it was opposed by New England and the cotton states—by New England, because she had so much money invested in slave ships, and by the cotton states because they wished more negroes for their cotton fields. For this reason not till early in the nineteenth century was the trade forbidden by law; and even after this it was for a time carried on secretly.

Change of Feeling in the North in regard to Slavery.—So long as the New England people were engaged in the slave trade, they did not take an active stand against slavery; but soon after the importation of negroes was stopped by law, the belief that slavery was an evil that should not exist in the country at all began to win adherents. The inhabitants of the North had nothing to lose by the destruction of the institution; for it had never gained any foothold among them, and had practically been abolished by the beginning of the nineteenth century.

Gabriel's Insurrection. — The negroes in Virginia were kindly treated by their masters, and as a rule gave but little trouble from insubordination. Several servile insurrections, however, mar the history of the commonwealth. The first occurred in 1800, and was instigated by a negro, named Gabriel, who belonged to a farmer near Richmond. He formed a plot to capture Richmond, kill the citizens, and plunder the place. He collected his followers, armed them with scythe blades, and set out on his nefarious expedition on a dark summer night. But he was doomed to disaster from the beginning. A violent storm made a creek in his front impassable, which delayed his operations. Before he could make his proposed attack, he learned that his plot had been discovered; and thereupon he and his deluded companions at once fled to the woods and swamps for refuge. Gabriel was captured, and with a number of others was condemned to death.

Nat Turner's Insurrection. — Thirty-one years later the tranquillity of the state was disturbed by a second insurrection, which resulted more seriously. A negro preacher by the name of Nat Turner, who belonged to a Mr. Travis of Southampton County, succeeded in persuading his people that he was a prophet. He appealed to their superstitions by tracing on a sheet of paper in blood a crucifix, a representation of the sun, and other mystic signs, which he claimed indicated the approach of the most remarkable events. As a result of his intriguing, the negroes all through the South Side fell under his influence and became frenzied with excitement. When his plot was ripe, he started the insurrection in Southampton County, by killing his master and family with an ax. Next a lady and ten children were slain, and then a number of school children. Now reveling in blood, and half crazy with excitement, the negroes marched to Jerusalem, now called Courtland, where they were dispersed by a party of armed citizens. They hid in the woods and swamps, where some were killed and the rest captured. Twenty-one were brought to Jerusalem for trial, and thirteen of them, Nat Turner among the number, were hanged. Fifty-five white persons, nearly all of whom were women and children, were the victims of this uprising.

Sentiment in Virginia in Later Times. — The feeling which Virginia had repeatedly manifested against slavery

continued.   In 1832 an emancipation bill was introduced
in the legislature.   The measure did not pass; but a
resolution, postponing the consideration of the matter till
public opinion had further developed, was adopted.   Had
Virginia been let alone and no attempt been mad? to inter-
fere with her domestic matters, she would doubtless have,
in due time, set her slaves free in a manner that would
have been best for them and for her own welfare.

Fugitive Slaves. — The Federal Constitution recognized
slavery fully, and it contained a provision that negroes
who might escape from their homes and go into another
state should be returned to their masters.   To carry out
this provision effectually, Congress passed a special law
that all runaway negroes found in the Northern states
should be arrested and, without trial by jury, be sent back
to their masters.   But the execution of this law was resisted
in the North, and in a number of states Personal Liberty
Laws were passed which nullified the act of Congress.

John Brown's Raid. — The excitement over slavery was
greatly intensified by an attempt that was made to bring
about the emancipation of the negroes of Virginia by incit-
ing them to raise an insurrection.   This was the act of
John Brown, a native of Connecticut, who had taken part
in the struggle in Kansas to keep that state from adopting
a constitution authorizing slavery.   On the night of October
16, 1859, he, with twenty followers, took possession of
Harper's Ferry, captured a number of citizens whom he
held as hostages, and seized the United States arsenal at
the place, intending to obtain from it arms for the negroes
whom he expected to join him.   But in this he was mistaken, for none of them came to his support.

Brown Captured and Executed. — Governor Wise called
out a force of volunteers and militia to put down the dis-

Capture of John Brown

turbance. But before the state troops could reach Har-per's Ferry, a number of Brown's gang had been killed and the rest captured by Colonel Robert E. Lee [1] and a body

[1] Robert E. Lee (1807–1870), born at Stratford, Westmoreland County, Va., descended from a long line of illustrious ancestors. He was educated at West Point; and, while there, he was never reprimanded, and never received a demerit. After his graduation, he served in the Mexican War, and rose to distinction. When Virginia seceded, Lee at once resigned his commission in the United States army and offered his services to his native state. His masterly defence of Richmond won for him a wide reputation as one of the ablest military commanders of modern times. When the Civil War ended, he was elected president of Washington College. After his death, in honor of him, the name of the college was changed to Washington and Lee University.

Lee was a strikingly handsome man and a graceful rider. His noble qualities and the great purity of his life made him an inspiration to his followers. In his own life, he certainly exemplified his belief in the maxim he himself uttered that " Duty is the sublimest word in the English language."

of United States marines, who had been dispatched to the scene of action. Several citizens and one negro were killed by Brown's party before the termination of the affair. Brown was among those captured, and he with six of his followers were tried and hung for treason, insurrection, and murder.

Report of the Senate Committee. — A committee of the United States Senate looked into the matter, and made a report in which it was stated that Brown's attack upon Virginia "was, simply the act of lawless ruffians, under the sanction of no public or political authority, distinguishable only from ordinary felonies by the ulterior ends in contemplation by them, and by the fact that the money to maintain the expedition and the large armament they brought with them had been contributed and furnished by the citizens of other states of the Union under circumstances that must continue to jeopard the safety and peace of the Southern states, and against which Congress has no power to legislate."

Political Significance of Brown's Attack. — Brown brought with him to Harper's Ferry a number of muskets, pistols, and about fifteen hundred pikes which were made expressly for him in Connecticut, and which he thought would be effective weapons in the hands of the negroes. An investigation of the insurrection showed that Brown had the sympathy and the help of a number of persons at the North in this plot to raise a servile war. This fact convinced Virginia that the Constitution and the laws of the Union were not sufficient to protect her, and it hastened the breaking out of the Civil War.

QUESTIONS

1. Why did England encourage the traffic in negroes?
2. What did Virginia do to prevent its growth?
3. What was New England's connection with slavery?
4. Why was it encouraged both by the New England and cotton states?
5. What change of feeling in regard to slavery had taken place in the North?
6. Give an account of Gabriel's Insurrection.
7. Of Nat Turner's Insurrection.
8. What was the sentiment in Virginia in later times?
9. What is said of fugitive slaves?
10. Who was John Brown, and what is said of his raid?
11. By whom was he captured?
12. Give the leading facts in the life of Robert E. Lee.
13. What was Brown's fate?
14. Give the report of the Senate Committee on this raid.
15. What weapons did John Brown bring, who were they for. and where made?
16. What did an investigation show?

REVIEW QUESTIONS

1. Describe the battles of King's Mountain and Cowpens.
2. Give an account of the maneuvers of Cornwallis and Lafayette.
3. How was Cornwallis entrapped?
4. Describe the siege of Yorktown and Cornwallis's surrender.
5. Who was Governor Nelson, and what is said of his patriotism?
6. Give an account of the exploits of George Rogers Clark, by which Virginia recovered her Northwest Territory.
7. What generous spirit did Virginia show in order to bring about a union of the states?
8. Why was the present Constitution formed to take the place of the Articles of Confederation?
9. Describe the Alien and Sedition Laws, and tell of the resolutions adopted by Virginia in regard to them.
10. Why is Virginia called the "Mother of States and of Statesmen"?
11. Describe the burning of Richmond theater.
12. What was the cause of the War of 1812?

VIRG. HIST. — 12

13. What important services did Virginians render the Union?
14. What was Virginia's attitude toward slavery?
15. Give New England's connection with slavery, and tell about the change of feeling at the North in regard to it.
16. What is said of fugitive slaves?
17. Give an account of John Brown's Raid, his capture and execution.
18. What was the report of the Senate Committee, and the political significance of this raid?

CHRONOLOGICAL TABLE OF IMPORTANT EVENTS (1763-1860)

1765. Stamp Act passed by Parliament.
1766. Stamp Act repealed.
1767. A tax imposed on tea and other articles.
1769. Famous Virginia resolves passed by the House of Burgesses.
1770. All duties except on tea repealed.
1773. The tea thrown overboard at Boston Harbor.
1774. The first Continental Congress met at Philadelphia, September 5
1775. Battles of Lexington and Concord, April 19.
1775. End of royal government in Virginia.
1775. Battle of Bunker Hill, June 17.
1776. Declaration of Independence signed, July 4.
1777. Burgoyne's surrender, October 17.
1778. American independence acknowledged by France.
1779. Clark's conquest of the Northwest Territory.
1780. Battle of King's Mountain, October 7.
1781. Richmond captured by Arnold.
1781. Battle of Cowpens, January 17.
1781. Surrender of Cornwallis, October 19.
1787. Constitution of the United States adopted in convention, September 17.
1788. Virginia ratifies the Constitution.
1789. Washington inaugurated, April 30.
1799. Washington died at Mt. Vernon, December 14.
1803. Louisiana purchased from France, April 30.
1811. Richmond theater burned, December 26.
1812. War declared against England.
1846. Mexican War.
1859. John Brown's Raid, October 16.

THIRD PERIOD—FROM THE CIVIL WAR TO THE PRESENT TIME

CHAPTER XXII

APPROACH OF THE CIVIL WAR

The Constitution Ambiguous. — The Constitution of the United States was the result of a series of compromises; and at the time of its adoption, was not entirely satisfactory to any one. No sooner had it been ratified by the states than the people became divided into two parties, one holding that the language of the Constitution should be construed strictly so that the sovereignty of the states would never be impaired, the other claiming that the powers of the Federal government ought to be enlarged, and that the Constitution should be interpreted so as to allow this to be done. Out of these antagonistic views there grew, as time passed, two opposing theories of the nature of the Union. These must now be stated in order to make clear the cause of the secession movement, which involved Virginia and all the other states in a long and bloody war.

The State-Rights Theory. — On this theory the Union which the states created was one of limited powers, all powers not named in the Constitution as specially surrendered to the Federal government being reserved by the states. Accordingly, the United States was not a nation like England, but a league or confederacy between thirteen separate peoples. The Union being thus in the nature of a partnership, not limited in time, it followed, by the law governing such agreements, that the right to withdraw remained with each state.

The National Theory. — The advocates of the second theory, called the National theory, held that the states in ratifying the Constitution had surrendered their statehood and had formed a nation. According to this view, the Union was indissoluble, and no state had a right to withdraw without the consent of the other states.

Which was the True Theory? — The interpretation that was given to the Constitution at the time of its formation is not historically uncertain. The evidence, if carefully examined, is convincing that the Union was regarded as a league. Mr. Lodge, a Northern writer, who has made a careful study of the subject, says: "When the Constitution was adopted by the votes of States at Philadelphia, and accepted by the votes of States in popular conventions, it is safe to say that there was not a man in the country, from Washington and Hamilton on the one side to George Clinton and George Mason on the other, who regarded the new system as anything but an experiment entered upon by the States, and from which each and every State had the right peaceably to withdraw, a right which was very likely to be exercised." The above quotation states correctly the view taken of the Union when it was made. It was considered a league formed by independent states, each one of which retained the attribute of sovereignty.[1]

---

[1] The advocates of the National theory of the Union often point to the clauses in the Constitution which forbid a state to make treaties, to coin money, to declare war, etc., as proof that the states surrendered their sovereignty.

The First Threats of Secession. — The first threats of secession came, not from the South, but from New England; and during the latter part of the eighteenth century and early in the nineteenth, movements were projected to bring about the withdrawal of New England from the Union. In 1796 Governor Wolcott of Connecticut declared that he wished the Northern states, the moment Jefferson was elected President, would separate from the Southern. The War of 1812 was very unpopular in New England, and while it was going on secession from the Union was openly urged in public meetings by prominent men.

Virginia and the South. — From the beginning Virginia had adopted the State-Rights theory of the Union, and she held to it unwaveringly. She formed no new political theories, but continued to look upon the Union as a league

But this argument loses its force, so far as the thirteen original states are concerned, from the fact that the restrictions mentioned were not laid on these states by any power above them or outside of them, but were self-imposed. Thus these clauses in the Constitution were similar in nature to those found in business contracts, by which the members of a firm agree to give up certain rights while they are in partnership; but when the compact between them is dissolved they can freely exercise the rights temporarily waived and all others that belong to individuals.

In speaking of the character of the Federal government Woodrow Wilson says : "To us of the present day it seems that the Constitution framed in 1787 gave birth in 1789 to a national government such as that which now constitutes an indestructible bond of union for the states; but the men of that time would certainly have laughed at any such idea." . . . "It was for his state, each man felt, that his blood and treasure had been poured out; it was that Massachusetts and Virginia might be free that the war (Revolution) had been fought, not that the colonies might have a new central government set up over them; patriotism was state patriotism. The states were living organic persons; the Union was an arrangement, — possibly it would prove to be only a temporary arrangement; new adjustments might have to be made." — See *State and Federal Governments of the United States*, pp. 28, 29.

between independent states. The South, without exception, under the teaching of John C. Calhoun, held to the same conception of the Federal tie. To Virginia and the South, therefore, the right to withdraw from the Union was one of the reserved rights of the states. Indeed, Virginia adopted the Constitution with the express understanding that she could reassume the powers she had delegated to the Federal government whenever these powers should be perverted to the injury or oppression of her people. Thus before she entered the Union she made clear her right to leave it.

The North and the West. — As times changed, the North changed its conception of what the Union was, and gave to the Constitution a meaning which no one attached to it in the early days of the republic. At first those who wished a strong government only held that the United States *ought to be* a nation. But under the influence of Daniel Webster the people of the North adopted the belief that the United States *was* a nation. Thus they changed the original conception of the Federal tie, and held that the states, in ratifying the Constitution, had formed a Union that could not be broken. The people of the West generally held the same political belief. It was natural that they should do this; for the Western states were created out of the public domain by the government of the United States, and for this reason, in them state lines did not have the same meaning as they did in the South, nor did state pride have the same influence. There was, it is true, much difference of opinion at the North and West upon the question of state sovereignty, many eminent statesmen and jurists viewing the matter as the South did; but on the whole the mass of the people at the North and West, under the influence of the new theory they had formed, regarded secession as unlawful and as constituting rebellion.

Reasons why the South wished to Secede. — The South and the North had not only grown apart in their political beliefs, but their interests had become different. The South was agricultural, while the North was largely engaged in manufacturing. Laws that suited one section did not suit the other, and this led to much irritation. The great cause of difference, however, was slavery, which had made the sections hostile to each other. The South, since slavery had become her peculiar institution, demanded that property in negroes should be as securely guaranteed as other forms of property, and desired to have slavery further extended. Adequate protection for this form of property the North was unwilling to give, as was shown in the way some of the states refused to allow the execution of the Fugitive Slave Law. , This rendered the South uneasy. The Federal government had been created by the states to give security against domestic, as well as foreign dangers. But the time had come when it no longer brought domestic peace. The rights, guaranteed to the South in regard to her slaves, had already been violated, and were threatened with further invasion in the future. It could no longer be said that the Constitution was a Magna Charta that preserved rights. The realization of this made the South desire to leave the Union. Under the same government, the people of the South and of the North had lived together as brothers for many years; but the state of feeling between them had now become very different from what it was in the days of the Revolution. It must ever be considered most deplorable that the people of the two sections should have become enemies ready to take each other's lives.

QUESTIONS

1. Was the Constitution of the United States satisfactory to all?
2. What two parties sprang up, and what was the result?
3. Give the State-Rights theory of the Union.
4. The National theory.
5. Which was the true one?
6. What does Mr. Lodge say on the subject?
7. From what section did the first threats of secession come?
8. What did the governor of Connecticut declare?
9. Which theory did Virginia hold of the Union?
10. With what express understanding had she adopted the Constitution?
11. By whose influence did the North change the original conception of the Federal tie?
12. Why did the people of the West hold the same opinion as the North?
13. In what ways were the interests of the North and South opposed?
14. What was the chief cause of the difference in the sections, and what is said of it?
15. Why did the South now feel uneasy in the Union?
16. What is said of the Constitution?

CHAPTER XXIII

THE BEGINNING OF THE CIVIL WAR

Secession of the Cotton States. — In 1860 Abraham Lincoln [1] was elected President by the Republican party, which
was opposed to any extension of slavery, and whose extreme members wished to abolish it in the territory where
it then existed. When this occurred, the cotton states
gave up hope of enjoying longer fraternal union with the
North, and decided to exercise their reserved right of
secession, thinking that this course of action was best for
their peace and prosperity. South Carolina acted first,
passing an ordinance of secession on December 20, 1860.
She was followed by Florida, Mississippi, Alabama, Georgia, Louisiana, and Texas. The movement proceeded
quietly, due observance being paid to legal form. The
seceded states then formed a new union, called the Con-

[1] Abraham Lincoln (1809-1865) was born in Kentucky. His parents were
of humble origin, and too poor to educate him. He attended school one year
only, and after this educated himself. When he was seven years old, his
father moved to Indiana, where he spent his early life in hardship and toil.
In 1830, the Lincoln family went to Illinois; and, on this journey, young
Lincoln walked the whole distance, driving an ox team. He then helped his
father build a log cabin, and split rails to inclose a little farm. In 1834, he
began to study law, and by borrowing books soon acquired knowledge enough
to be admitted to the bar. He next turned his attention to politics; and,
after this, his life was a succession of promotions. He was elected to the
Legislature, then to Congress, and, in 1860, we find him President of the
United States. He was noted for rugged strength of character, his friends
calling him " Honest Abe."

Abraham Lincoln

federate States of America, with Jefferson Davis[1] of Mississippi as president.

Virginia's Effort for Peace. — For a time there was a prospect of bringing the sections together again, and Virginia earnestly desired to do this. She believed in the right of secession, but she doubted the expediency of the act. In addition to this, she was deeply attached to the Union for whose establishment she had done so much. Animated by her love for it, she, through her General Assembly, at the suggestion of John Tyler, formerly President of the United States, called for a Peace Conference to be participated in by all the states. This conference, which met in Washington, and was presided over by Ex-President Tyler, failed in its efforts to restore harmony.

Diplomacy. — After the inauguration of President Lincoln, the Confederate government sent commissioners to Washington to arrange for a peaceable settlement of all questions at issue between the two governments. One thing asked for was the evacuation of all the forts in the territory of the seceded states that were still in possession of the United States. Fort Sumter in Charleston harbor was one of these; and Mr. Seward, Secretary of State under Lincoln, gave assurance[2] that the fort would be

[1] Jefferson Davis (1808–1889) was a Kentuckian by birth, but when he was a few years old his father moved to Mississippi. He graduated at the United States Military Academy, after which he served for five years in the Indian wars in the West. He then resigned his commission in the army and became a cotton planter in Mississippi. He was elected to Congress ; but resigned his seat to serve in the Mexican War, in which he rose to distinction. Later he was elected to the United States Senate. On the formation of the Southern Confederacy he was elected president, and he filled this office till the end of the Civil War. He died in Mississippi in 1889.

[2] The assurance that Fort Sumter would be evacuated was given by Mr. Seward to Judge Campbell, who conveyed the information to the commissioners. See "Three Decades of Federal Legislation," by S. S. Cox, pp. 147, 148.

speedily given up. But this was not done; and after some delay Governor Pickens of South Carolina was notified from Washington that the fort would be reënforced "peaceably if permitted, forcibly if necessary," by a fleet that was then on its way.

Capture of Fort Sumter. — The Confederate government, accepting the message to Governor Pickens as a declaration of war, ordered General Beauregard, who was in command of the Southern troops at Charleston, to demand the surrender of Fort Sumter. Major Anderson, the commander of the Federal garrison, refused to evacu-

Fort Sumter

ate the fort; and thereupon Beauregard bombarded it and captured it on April 14, 1861.

War now Inevitable. — The crisis had at last come. The Confederates held that the North had acted in regard to Fort Sumter so as to render the use of force by the South necessary, and was for this reason the real aggressor, while the North contended that the South had by firing on the fort begun the war. Thus each section charged the other with bringing on the conflict. The cotton states had already made some preparations for war; and now all over the South the cry, "To arms! To arms!" was heard. The people of the North on their part came strongly to the support of the new Republican administration, and responded

Jefferson Davis

with alacrity to a call made by President Lincoln, during the excitement following the bombardment, for seventy-five thousand troops to reëstablish the Federal authority in the Southern states.

Secession of Virginia. — When President Lincoln called for troops, Virginia had to decide whether she would remain in the Union or join the Southern Confederacy. Up to this time she had steadily refused to secede. A convention, which had been called in view of the impending crisis, had refused to pass an ordinance of secession by a vote of eighty-nine to forty-five; but two days after Lincoln called for troops, this same convention passed the ordinance by a vote of eighty-eight to fifty-five. When the ordinance was submitted to the people, it was ratified by a large majority, and the state took her place in the Southern Confederacy.

Her Heroic Action. — This was Virginia's decision when called upon to help make war upon the states further south. She took her action deliberately, well knowing that she would be attacked on the north, east, and west, and would be the battlefield of a war which, if long continued, would be most destructive to her prosperity, let the end be what it might. There is recorded in history no greater act of self-sacrifice than that of Virginia in withdrawing from a Union she did not wish to leave, in order to help other states defend what she had always maintained was her right and theirs.

Actions of Other States. — Virginia's example in leaving the Union was followed by Arkansas, Tennessee, and North Carolina. Kentucky wished to remain neutral, but was overrun by Federal troops. So altogether eleven states seceded and twenty-three remained in the Union.

Return of Virginians. — In the Federal army and navy there were a number of distinguished Virginia officers,

who, at the opening of the war, had to determine to which
side they should render allegiance.   There were but few
who did not decide that
after their state had left
the Union they no longer
owed fealty to the United
States.   So there was a
return of Virginians to defend their native land.
Some had already distin-
guished themselves in the
service of the United
States, but were destined
to win yet greater military
renown in the Civil War.
**Distinguished Leaders
who came to Virginia.** —
Among those who resigned
commissions in the United States army were General
Albert Sidney Johnston,[1] the commander of the military
district of the Pacific, and that able and cautious soldier,
General Joseph E. Johnston,[2] who became the first com-

Joseph E. Johnston

[1] Albert Sidney Johnston (1803-1862) was born in Kentucky, but was of
New England descent. In his early life, he was described as "a handsome,
proud, manly, earnest, and self-reliant boy." He was educated at West Point,
where he showed great talent for mathematics. He served with distinction
in the Black Hawk war and in the Texas war for independence. When General Johnston reached Richmond, he was assigned by President Davis to the
command of the Confederate forces in the West. In 1862, he was wounded
in the battle of Shiloh and bled to death upon the field. In his death the
Confederacy sustained a severe loss. He was a man of courteous manners
and of noble and commanding appearance.

[2] Joseph E. Johnston (1807-1891), born in Prince Edward County, Va.,
was the youngest son of Major Peter Johnston of the Revolution. He
was educated at West Point, and served with distinction in the Mexican

mander of the Confederate army in Virginia. But the greatest of all the men who came to the help of Virginia in her hour of need was Colonel Robert E. Lee, a son of Light Horse Harry Lee of Revolutionary fame. In resigning his commission in the United States army, he used the often-quoted expression, "Save in the defense of my native state, I never desire again to draw my sword." In speaking of his decision in a letter, written to his sister, he says, "With all my devotion to the Union and the feeling of loyalty and duty as an American citizen, I have not been able to make up my mind to raise my hand against my relatives, my children, my home." When Colonel Lee reached Richmond, he was at once made commander of the Virginia forces.

Military Ardor. — All through the part of Virginia east of the Alleghany Mountains the people gave themselves up to preparations for war. Everywhere military companies were organized and equipped. Drill masters soon became so much in demand that Major Thomas J. Jackson, a professor in the Virginia Military Institute, was ordered to bring a number of cadets to Richmond to assist in the work of drilling recruits at Camp Lee. Jackson never returned to his quiet professorial duties. He was appointed a colonel of volunteers by the governor of Virginia and soon after entered upon a career of fame second only to that of General Lee.

Virginia Dismembered. — Western Virginia was opposed to leaving the Union, and refused to be bound by the action

War. In the early part of the Civil War he was commander of all the Confederate forces in Virginia. In the battle of Seven Pines he was severely wounded; and, when he reported for duty again, he was put in command of the military district of Tennessee. He continued to serve the Confederacy in the Southern campaigns till the close of the war. He is justly regarded as one of the ablest generals on the Confederate side.

of the convention that passed the ordinance of secession. So the people of this section in a convention held on June 11, 1861, organized a government of their own; and at a later period this part of the Old Dominion was admitted by Congress into the Union as a separate state, though a strained interpretation[1] had to be put upon the Constitution to bring this about. Thus the Virginia that took part in the War of Secession was in area about the same as the Virginia that helped to carry on the Revolution.

QUESTIONS

1. Who was elected President by the Republican party in 1860?
2. Give the leading facts of his life, and state the policy of his party.
3. After his election, what did the cotton states decide to do?
4. What union did they form, and whom did they elect president?
5. Give the leading facts in the life of Jefferson Davis.
6. Why did Virginia earnestly desire peace, and what action did she take to bring it about?
7. For what purpose did the Confederate government send commissioners to Washington after Lincoln's inauguration?
8. What particular request did they make? Was it granted?
9. What notification was sent to Governor Pickens in regard to Fort Sumter?
10. How did the Confederate government accept this notification, and what happened?
11. On what grounds did each section charge the other with beginning the war?
12. Why did Lincoln issue a call for seventy-five thousand troops?
13. Why did Virginia secede?

[1] The government organized by the people of West Virginia had, when it was first formed, jurisdiction over only 282,000 of the 1,600,000 inhabitants of Virginia. But those who adhered to it claimed that it was the true and lawful government of Virginia; and their legislature authorized the formation of a new state. This action the Federal government accepted as representing the consent of Virginia to the division of her territory; and so West Virginia was admitted as a separate state.

14. What is said of her heroic action in so doing?
15. Name the states that followed her example.
16. What is said of the return of Virginians?
17. What distinguished generals of the Federal army came to Virginia?
18. Give the leading facts in the life of Albert Sidney Johnston.
19. Of Joseph E. Johnston.
20. What did Robert E. Lee say on resigning his commission in the Federal army?
21. Describe the military ardor throughout Virginia.
22. When and why was the state of West Virginia formed?

CHAPTER XXIV

THE FIRST MOVEMENT AGAINST RICHMOND

Events that will be Recorded. — The military operations in the Civil War were on a very extensive scale. The struggle was prosecuted vigorously on both sides, not only in Virginia, but also in the South and West. In this short history, only a brief account of the leading military operations that took place in Virginia can be given.

"On to Richmond!" — On May 21, the capital of the Southern Confederacy was moved from Montgomery, Alabama, to Richmond; and at once in the North the cry of "On to Richmond!" was raised. The formation of Federal armies for the invasion of Virginia went on at different points. One gathered at Washington under General Scott, with General McDowell in immediate command, a second at Chambersburg under General Patterson, a third in West Virginia under General McClellan, and a fourth at Fortress Monroe under General Butler. To capture Richmond and bring the war to a speedy end was the plan of the Federals.

Preparations for Defense. — The Confederates collected troops for the protection of Virginia, and able plans for defense were adopted. General Beauregard [1] organized an

---

[1] Pierre Gustave Toutant Beauregard (1818–1893) was born in Louisiana. He was the son of a wealthy cotton planter, and was of French extraction. He was lively in temperament, possessed courteous manners, and showed good breeding and education. He was so fortunate in his military operations that the *Richmond Examiner* gave him the title "Beauregard Felix."

army at Manassas Junction to guard the direct approach from Washington to Richmond; General Joseph E. Johnston a second at Harper's Ferry to cover the Shenandoah valley; Generals Huger and Magruder a third to bar the route to Richmond by way of the peninsula between the James and the York rivers, while General Garnett was sent with troops to West Virginia to operate against the Federals in that part of the state.

Opening of Hostilities in Virginia. — The first invasion of the state occurred on May 24, 1861, when Federal troops took possession of Alexandria, where there were a number of strong secessionists. For some days before the occupation, a Confederate flag flying from the top of a hotel had been plainly seen from the President's house in Washington. This, Colonel Ellsworth of the Fire Zouave Regiment, U. S. A., hastened to take down with his own hand. But as he descended from the top of the building, holding the flag, he was shot dead by the owner, Mr. Jackson, who was himself killed a moment later by Ellsworth's soldiers. This was the first bloodshed in Virginia, and the next took place in a skirmish at Big Bethel, near Fortress Monroe, on June 10, when fourteen hundred Confederates under General John B. Magruder defeated three thousand Federals, belonging to the army of General Butler. These events mark the opening of the great struggle that took place in Virginia.

Battle of Manassas. — But the first important battle of the war took place at Manassas, where an army of thirty thousand Federals under General McDowell, which had set out from Washington for Richmond, encountered the Confederate army under General Beauregard. As the left wing of the Federal army attempted to cross Bull Run, a little stream that flows along the plains of Manassas, a skirmish occurred in which the Federals were driven back. This was but the forerunner of a general engagement which took place on July 21, 1861.   In this battle success was at first with the Federals.   Their right wing drove back the left wing of the Confederates, which rendered

Stonewall Jackson in the Battle of Manassas

the situation full of peril.   Seeing this General Bee of South Carolina rushed up to General Thomas J. Jackson,[1]

[1] Thomas Jonathan Jackson (1824-1863), was born at Clarksburg, Va. His father died when he was but three years old.   When he grew up he secured an appointment to the United States Military Academy, where he graduated in 1846.   In the Mexican War he showed such daring and bravery in the assault on the castle of Chapultepec that he was highly praised by his superior officers.   In 1851, he resigned from the army to accept a professorship in the Virginia Military Academy.   In July, 1861, he was made a brigadier general in the Confederate army.   He possessed a very strong individuality,

and exclaimed, "General, they are beating us back!" "Sir, we will give them the bayonet," was Jackson's prompt reply. Bee went back to his men and rallied them, saying, "Look, there is Jackson standing like a stone wall. Let us determine to die here, and we will conquer." From that day General Jackson became known to fame as Stonewall Jackson.

The Confederates rallied after the day seemed about lost, and checked the advance of the Federals till Kirby Smith, who had been sent by General Johnston from the Valley, arrived with reënforcements which made Beauregard's army nearly equal in numbers to McDowell's. Then the tide of battle turned, and the Federals began a retreat which ended in a rout and a panic. The soldiers threw away their arms and fled toward Washington.

The Victory not Followed up. — The Confederates did not follow up their great victory. Indeed, they did not realize its completeness till the day after the battle. Had they pushed on with all speed after the terror-stricken Federals, they might perhaps have followed them over the bridge across the Potomac, for the destruction of which no preparations had been made, and taken possession of Washington. In not doing this, they lost an opportunity which never came to them again.

Situation at the End of 1861. — As the year drew to a close, it became evident that the war would not end in a short time as many had supposed. Both sides now pre-

and was one of the most remarkable men that fought on the Southern side. In his short but brilliant military career he won the respect and admiration of friends and foes alike. He was a man of deep moral earnestness and intense convictions, his motto being "Do your duty and leave the rest to Providence." It was said that he never entered upon a battle without first kneeling to invoke the aid and guidance of Almighty God.

pared for a prolonged contest. The Federal army at Washington, which was known as the Army of the Potomac, was greatly increased. General George B. McClellan was made its commander in place of General Scott; and during the autumn and winter his forces numbering nearly two hundred thousand lay around Washington. He was confronted by the Army of Northern Virginia about sixty thousand strong under General Joseph E. Johnston. After

Manassas the Confederates had advanced as far as Fairfax Courthouse, and the flags at their outposts were visible in Washington.

Resources of the Two Sections. — A brief comparison of the resources of the two sections is necessary to show the unequal character of the struggle in which the South was engaged. In round numbers the states that remained in the

Gen. George B. McClellan

Union had a population of twenty-three millions, while the territory of the Confederacy contained only nine millions, of which three and a half millions were negroes. So the North could put in the field more than three times as many soldiers as the South. Besides this, the North had factories of all kinds, and could manufacture all the war supplies, arms, and clothes that the soldiers would need. The South was almost without factories; and soon after the opening of hostilities, her ports were blockaded by the

North. Thus all help from abroad was cut off. But the victory at Manassas made the South believe that, in spite of her inferior resources, success would crown her arms. She had faith in her own prowess; and she hoped too that she would not have to contend against the United States unaided. England and France had promptly accorded her belligerent rights; and it seemed probable, early in the war, that these powers might even acknowledge her independence.

QUESTIONS

1. What action on the part of the Confederacy caused the cry of "On to Richmond!" to be raised by the North?
2. What preparations did the Federals make to invade Virginia?
3. How did the Confederates prepare to defend the state?
4. What incident caused the first bloodshed on her soil?
5. When and where did the first skirmish take place?
6. Give an account of the battle of Manassas.
7. How did Jackson receive the name of Stonewall?
8. Give the leading facts in the life of Stonewall Jackson.
9. What was the result of the battle of Manassas?
10. Had the Confederates followed up this victory, what might have been the result?
11. What was the condition of the two armies at the end of 1861?
12. Compare the resources of the two sections.

CHAPTER XXV

The *Virginia*. — After the secession of Virginia, the Federal navy yard at Norfolk fell into the hands of the Confederates. Before the Federals left it, however, they burned and sunk a number of vessels. Among these was a frigate, called the *Merrimac*, which was only partly destroyed. This the Confederates raised and covered heavily with iron, thus converting the wooden ship into a most formidable ironclad, the first that was ever made. On March 8, 1862, just before the land campaign opened, this strange-looking craft, which had been renamed *Virginia*, steamed into Hampton Roads and attacked the Federal fleet. The heaviest guns were brought to bear upon her, but they produced no impression whatever on her iron sides. She speedily sunk the *Cumberland* and the *Congress*, while the *Minnesota*, in trying to escape, ran aground. The rest of the fleet scattered.

Battle between the *Virginia* and the *Monitor*. — The *Virginia*, having won a complete triumph, went back to Norfolk when night came on, returning the next day to renew her attack on the *Minnesota*. But this time she was met by a formidable enemy that had arrived in the night. This was Ericsson's *Monitor*, an ironclad gunboat that looked like "a cheese box on a raft." A fierce engagement took place between the ironclads, but neither could seriously damage the other, and so the bat-

205

The *Cumberland* and the *Virginia*

tle was a drawn one. The appearance of the *Monitor*, however, was most opportune for the Federal cause; for had the *Virginia* been unopposed for a short time, she might have ascended the Potomac and destroyed Washington.

A little later the Confederates evacuated Norfolk; and the *Virginia* was blown up to keep her from falling into the hands of the Federals. Thus her career came to an end. The battle between the *Virginia* and the *Monitor* showed that in the future naval conflicts would be decided by ironclads, and it caused all the great powers to reconstruct their navies, thus producing a revolution in naval warfare.

Plan of the Peninsular Campaign. — When the spring opened, instead of attacking Johnston where he was, McClellan decided to transport his army by water to the peninsula between the James and the York rivers, and to approach Richmond from that direction. He was to be supported by reënforcements that were to proceed by land from Washington. The Confederates on their part arranged to have General Johnston march down from Manassas to oppose McClellan.

Jackson's Valley Campaign. — But Stonewall Jackson was left in the Valley of Virginia, where he carried on a campaign which for daring and brilliancy is surpassed by none recorded in history. He proved himself so active that he completely disarranged the Federal plans. His presence in the Valley put Washington in danger; and the Lincoln government decided that it was necessary to dislodge him or capture him before reënforcements could be sent to McClellan. But victory remained with Jackson. In three months — from the last of March to the last of June — he defeated and scattered four Federal armies under Milroy, Fremont, Banks, and Shields, winning every battle except one at Kernstown. With an army that never numbered more than seventeen thousand, he threw the whole North into a panic, and kept sixty thousand men from joining McClellan down on the peninsula. All this he accomplished with a total loss of less than two thousand. Jackson's exploits in this campaign won for him the admiration not only of America, but also of Europe.

Battle of Seven Pines. — While Jackson was operating in the Valley, McClellan started on his peninsular campaign. With a magnificent army of one hundred and ten thousand, a large number of transports, men-of-war, and vessels loaded with supplies, he landed at Old Point. General Magruder, with an army of eleven thousand, delayed his progress till Johnston came down from Manassas and threw his army between McClellan and Richmond. On May 31, 1862, at

Seven Pines, while the two wings of the Federal army were separated by the Chickahominy River, Johnston attacked McClellan, and defeating the left wing of his army, drove it back with heavy loss. The right wing of the Federal army held its ground, and this rendered the battle indecisive; but McClellan's advance was for the time stopped. In this engagement, Johnston was severely

The Seven Days' Battles

wounded; and he was succeeded by General Lee, who remained at the head of the Army of Northern Virginia till the end of the war.

The Seven Days' Battles. — General Lee called Jackson and his men who were flushed with their victories in the Valley to his aid, and from June 26 to July 2 fought the series of battles known as the Seven Days' Battles, in which he struck McClellan blow after blow. As a result of these engagements, the Federal commander was forced to withdraw his army from the vicinity of Richmond to the James River. The last of these battles was fought at Malvern Hill, where McClellan had taken a strong position. Here on July 1, the Confederates rashly attacked him, and were repulsed with heavy loss. They did not retire, however, when night came on, but remained close to the Federal fortifications, intending to renew the battle in the morning; but two hours after the Confederates had withdrawn from the attack, the Federals, under cover of darkness, made a hasty retreat to Harrison Landing, where the presence of their fleet rendered them safe from attack. In this campaign Lee's effective strength was eighty thousand, and McClellan's one hundred and five thousand. The result was a complete Confederate triumph. Richmond was saved and the North discouraged.

Second Manassas. — The peninsular campaign having proved a failure, the Federal army was transferred to Acquia Creek, and joined with the army in front of Washington. General Pope was put in command of the whole. He, when he entered upon his campaign, issued a proclamation in which he announced that success and glory were in the front, and that " his headquarters would be in the saddle." He did not, however, make much progress in his effort to capture Richmond. At Manassas, on August 29–30, he was defeated by Lee, and his army retreated in confusion to the defenses of Washington. The unfortunate Federal general was, after his defeat, sent off on an expedition against the Indians, and McClellan was restored to the command of the Federal army.

Invasion of Maryland. — While McClellan was engaged in reorganizing his army, Lee moved north into Maryland. When he reached Frederick, he divided his army and sent Jackson back to capture Harper's Ferry, which was strongly garrisoned by the Federals.   Unfortunately, a lost copy of Lee's orders, directing the movements of the Confederates on the Maryland campaign, fell into McClellan's hands, who, with the information he thus obtained, moved rapidly in the hope that he could crush Lee's forces while they were divided.   But Jackson promptly captured Harper's

Harper's Ferry

Ferry and rejoined General Lee before McClellan could carry out his plan.

Battle of Sharpsburg. — At Sharpsburg, on September 17, 1862, the Confederate army, numbering less than forty thousand, was attacked by McClellan with eighty-seven thousand men.   The Confederates fought magnificently, and throughout the entire day repelled every attack made upon them.   They maintained a defiant front all the next day, but neither side renewed the conflict, and when night came General Lee recrossed the Potomac into Virginia. Some Federal brigades followed the Confederates across the river, but these were attacked by General A. P. Hill,[1] who commanded Lee's rear guard, and driven back. Sharpsburg, or Antietam, as the engagement is named by Northern writers, is frequently called a drawn battle, but it had the effect of bringing the Confederate invasion of Maryland to an end, and of relieving the Federal authorities of the fears they entertained for the safety of Baltimore and Washington. The Confederates had crossed the Potomac singing " Maryland, my Maryland," and Lee expected that the Marylanders would come to him in large numbers, but in this he was disappointed, for but few recruits joined his standard.

A. P. Hill

Distinguished Englishmen Visit Lee. — General Lee remained for a few days in the neighborhood of Shepherdstown, and then took a position near Winchester, where he allowed his war-worn army to rest for a few weeks. During this period several distinguished British officers, among whom was Lord Wolseley, visited him at his headquarters.

[1] Ambrose Powell Hill (1825–1865) was born in Culpeper County, Va. He descended from a long line of patriotic ancestors. He was educated at West Point, and served in the Mexican War. At the breaking out of the Civil War he was chosen colonel of a Virginia regiment, and then was made brigadier general. In 1863, he was appointed lieutenant general. In many of the operations of the war he bore a gallant and conspicuous part. He was shot through the heart on April 2, 1865, during the final attack on Petersburg.

Battle of Fredericksburg. — Toward the end of October, General McClellan crossed the Potomac and began another invasion of Virginia. But he had not given satisfaction to the government at Washington, and so he was retired and General Burnside succeeded him. The new commander, at the head of one hundred and thirteen thousand men, made his advance toward Richmond by way of Fredericksburg, where he encountered Lee's army, numbering sixty-five thousand. On December 13 he attacked the Confederates and sustained a crushing defeat. In the "Horror of Fredericksburg," as the battle was called, the Federals lost nearly thirteen thousand and the Confederates about five thousand men. Burnside was now replaced by General Hooker, "Fighting Joe Hooker" he was called, and the Federals went into winter quarters at Falmouth.

QUESTIONS

1. Give the early history of the ironclad *Virginia*.
2. Describe the battle between the *Virginia* and the *Monitor*.
3. What was the fate of the *Virginia?*
4. What radical change in the navies of the world did this battle produce?
5. Give the plan of the Peninsular Campaign.
6. Give an account of Jackson's Valley Campaign.
7. How did Johnston check McClellan's advance at Seven Pines?
8. Who succeeded Johnston after this battle?
9. Describe the Seven Days' Battles.
10. What was the effective strength of the two armies?
11. What was the result of this campaign?
12. What proclamation did General Pope make?
13. What was the result of the second battle of Manassas?
14. What state did Lee now invade?
15. Describe the battle of Sharpsburg, and give its result.
16. Who visited Lee while his army was encamped near Winchester?
17. Describe the battle of Fredericksburg.

REVIEW QUESTIONS

1. What two theories were held in regard to the Constitution?
2. From what section did the first threats of secession come?
3. How did Virginia and the South look upon the Union?
4. How did the North and West regard it?
5. Give the reasons that made the South desire to leave the Union.
6. Who was elected President in 1860, and what followed his election?
7. What efforts did Virginia make for peace?
8. What request did the Confederate States make of the Federal government?
9. Give an account of the capture of Fort Sumter, and of the effect it had in the North and South.
10. What caused Virginia to secede, and what states followed her example?
11. Name some of the distinguished officers who resigned their commissions and came to Virginia.
12. What led to the formation of West Virginia?
13. What plans did the Federals make for invading Virginia, and how did the Confederates prepare to defend her?
14. Give an account of the opening of hostilities in Virginia.
15. Describe the battle of Manassas.
16. What was the situation in 1861, and how did the North and South compare in resources?
17. Describe the battle between the *Virginia* and the *Monitor*.
18. Give an account of Jackson's Valley Campaign.
19. Tell of the battle of Seven Pines.
20. Describe the Seven Days' Battles.
21. Tell of the second battle of Manassas.
22. What is said of Lee's invasion of Maryland?
23. Describe the battle of Sharpsburg or Antietam.
24. Give an account of the battle of Fredericksburg.

CHAPTER XXVI

Chancellorsville. — Not till April, 1863, was General Hooker ready to begin his campaign. Then he put in motion his army, numbering one hundred and thirty-two thousand men, ·"the finest army on the planet," he called it. He crossed the Rappahannock about twenty-five miles above Fredericksburg. Lee opposed him with sixty thousand men, and the two armies met at Chancellorsville on the 2nd of May. Jackson marched rapidly across the front of the Federal

Stonewall Jackson

army, and falling unexpectedly upon Hooker's right wing, drove it back in utter rout to Chancellorsville. The next day Lee forced Hooker back over the Rappahannock, and then turning on General Sedgwick, who with twenty-five thousand men had captured Marye's Heights, drove him likewise across the river. The result of the operations of four days from May 2 to May 5 was a total defeat of the Federal army, with a loss of seventeen thousand to twelve thousand of the Confederates.

Death of Stonewall Jackson. — But Chancellorsville was a dearly won victory to the Confederates, for on May 2, Stonewall Jackson, at the moment of victory, was accidentally shot by his own men as he returned from a reconnoissance. His injuries were so serious as to render the amputation of his arm necessary. After this had been done, pneumonia set in, and he died on May 10. " Let us cross over the river and rest in the shade of the trees," were the last words of this renowned soldier. " I have lost my right arm!" General Lee exclaimed, when he learned that Jackson was dead. For daring, swiftness in execution, untiring energy, and moral influence, Jackson stood preëminent. Never for a moment did he doubt that the Southern cause was righteous, or lose faith in its ultimate triumph. In his death the Confederates sustained an irreparable loss. His place could not be supplied. There was but one Stonewall Jackson.

Brandy Station. — When Lee's army began to move after the battle of Chancellorsville, Hooker sent his cavalry across the Rappahannock River to penetrate the designs of the Confederates. At Brandy Station, where the Federals encountered General Stuart,[1] the fiercest cavalry battle

J. E. B. Stuart

[1] James E. B. Stuart (1832–1864), was born in Virginia and served in the United States army on the frontier fighting Indians, where he became noted

of the whole war took place. Each side was about ten thousand strong. The engagement lasted all day, but ended in the defeat of the Federals, who, after sustaining a heavy loss, were forced to recross the river.

Battle of Gettysburg. — After the victory at Chancellorsville, Lee assumed the offensive and invaded Pennsylvania with an army seventy thousand strong. The Federal army, numbering one hundred and two thousand, under a new commander, General Meade, followed the Confederates. The foremost divisions of the opposing forces came together at Gettysburg. The Federals secured a position on some hills called Cemetery Ridge, where they fortified themselves strongly. Here General Lee attacked them, and for three days (July 1–3) a fierce battle raged. The turning point came on the third day when three Confederate divisions, Pickett's, Pettigrew's, and Pender's, numbering fifteen thousand in all, made a desperate charge on the Federal left center under a fire more severe than that which opened on the Old Guard at Waterloo. The divisions of Pettigrew and Pender recoiled under the terrible cannonade to which they were subjected ; but Pickett's division, composed of Virginia veterans, kept on as steadily as men on parade, broke through the Federal lines and planted their colors within them. Had they been properly supported, they would have won a decisive victory. But no support came, and the gallant division, after holding on alone for ten minutes, was cut to pieces and forced to retire, after having made a charge that surpassed that of the famous Light Brigade at Balaklava. Both armies

for his daring. In 1861 he was appointed by Lincoln a captain in the United States cavalry, but he declined the appointment to enter the Confederate service. He was the most dashing officer in the Confederate cavalry. He fell at *Yellow Tavern*, May, 1864.

suffered severely, the Confederate loss being twenty thousand and the Federal twenty-three thousand men. General Lee, having failed in his attempt to drive the Federals from their fortified heights, took a position a few miles from Meade's army, where he remained for ten days, and then retired across the Potomac into Virginia.

The Turning Point in the War.— Gettysburg, though not a decisive victory like Waterloo, marks the turning point in the Civil War. Had Lee been able to overthrow the Federal army on that hard-fought field, it might have brought peace. Gregg, the English historian, says he was assured on what seemed to be sufficient authority, that if Lee had been victorious at Gettysburg, the government of England was prepared to join with France in recognizing the Confederate States as an independent power. There was now, however, but little hope of foreign intervention. Serious disasters had already befallen the Confederate armies in the South and West. The day after Gettysburg the fall of Vicksburg gave the Federals control of the Mississippi River, and by the end of the year, 1863, much of the territory of the Confederacy had fallen into the hands of the Federals. Still there was hope of ultimate success as long as the Army of Northern Virginia was in the field. By this time Lee had become the idol of the South. He had won the confidence and love of the people, and to him and his army they looked for deliverance.

QUESTIONS

1. Describe the battle of Chancellorsville.
2. Why was it a dearly won victory for the Confederates?
3. Give an account of the death of Stonewall Jackson.
4. What did General Lee exclaim on hearing of it?
5. What is said of Jackson?

6. Who was J. E. B. Stuart, and what fierce cavalry battle did he win?
7. What Northern state did Lee invade after the battle of Chancellorsville?
8. By whom was he followed, and what was the relative strength of the two armies?
9. Describe the battle of Gettysburg.
10. What is said of Pickett's division at Gettysburg?
11. What was the result of this battle?
12. Why is Gettysburg regarded as the turning point of the war?
13. What disasters had befallen the Confederacy in the South and West?
14. To whom did the South look for ultimate success?

CHAPTER XXVII

LEE AND GRANT

The Raid of Kilpatrick and Dahlgren. — In March 1864, the Federal authorities dispatched General Kilpatrick with four thousand cavalry on a raid around Lee's lines, the object of which was to capture Richmond by a dash, and to release the prisoners confined there. Kilpatrick planned to make his attack from the north, and he sent Colonel Ulric Dahlgren with a detachment of his troops to approach the city from the south. But the expedition came to nothing. Dahlgren[1] was killed by the Confederates, and his command scattered, while Kilpatrick was forced to retreat. This bold attempt was made just before the opening of the spring campaign, in which Virginia was destined to become the battle ground of one of the most remarkable series of engagements recorded in history.

General Grant.[2] — During the first years of the war General Ulysses S. Grant, a resident of Illinois, rose to distinc-

[1] Upon Dahlgren's person orders instructing him to kill President Davis and to burn Richmond were found. These were photographed, and General Lee sent copies to General Meade, who in reply stated that no such orders had been given to Dahlgren. Admiral Dahlgren, in speaking of the occurrence says that, in the orders, his son's name was incorrectly spelled, and his explanation of the matter is that the orders were forgeries.

[2] Ulysses S. Grant (1822–1885), was born in Ohio, and descended from Scotch ancestry. He graduated at West Point, and served in the Mexican War, where he won promotion for gallant conduct. When this war ended, Grant retired to private life. At the breaking out of the Civil War, he raised a company of volunteers, and entered the Union service. In August, 1861, he was

tion in the operations that were carried on in the West and South. He was noted for his great ability to handle armies under difficult circumstances, and for the energy with which he threw himself into the contest. In March, 1864, he was put in command of all the forces of the United States, and took charge in person of the military operations in Virginia.

The "Hammering Campaign." — Grant became commander in chief of the Federal army at a time when the strength of the South was nearly exhausted. Realizing this, he decided to adopt the method of continuously hammering at the Confederates and their resources till the South should be compelled to submit. Thus his policy was to trust to force rather than to strategy. The Hammering campaign for Virginia, planned by Grant, was very extensive. The Army of the Potomac was to advance from the north on Richmond. General Butler was to move up the James with a fleet and some thirty-five thousand men, capture Petersburg, and attack Richmond from the south, while Generals Crook and Sigel were to operate in the Valley, and, after taking Staunton and Lynchburg, to attack the Confederates in the rear. The movements of the Army of the Potomac General Grant directed himself, though General Meade was left in immediate command.

Battles of the Wilderness. — When the campaign opened, the Army of the Potomac numbered one hundred and

made a brigadier general. He won his great reputation as the successful leader of the Federal armies. After the war, he was elected by the Republican party President of the United States, and filled this high office at a time when strength of character was much needed in solving the difficult problems of Reconstruction. At the close of his second term, he made a tour around the world; and, by the governments of foreign countries, he was everywhere treated with the highest honor.

U. S. Grant

eighteen thousand, and it was opposed by General Lee with about sixty-four thousand, according to the highest estimates. Grant crossed the Rapidan on his march southward, and entered a region of country covered with scraggy oak and pine trees and full of tangled under-brush, known as the Wilderness. Here, not far from Chancellorsville, the hostile armies came into collision, and for five days a terrible contest went on; but Grant was unable to drive Lee back. By moving to the left, however, he reached Spottsylvania Courthouse where much heavy fighting took place. A flank movement brought Grant to Cold Harbor, where, early in June, in attempting to carry the Confederate works by assault, he lost thirteen thousand men in a half hour, and his men refused to renew the attack. Grant again moved to the left and crossed the James, having resolved to lay siege to Petersburg.

Lee's Generalship. — General Lee's management of this campaign alone would have rendered him famous. In the long series of engagements that took place from the Wilderness to the James, he had defeated his powerful antagonist again and again, and inflicted on him a loss that exceeded the total number of his own forces. Not only did he do this, but in spite of all the difficulties that surrounded him, he succeeded in keeping the expeditions that were to coöperate with the Army of the Potomac from rendering any very effective aid. The chief results of these minor campaigns were as follows.

Butler Imprisoned. — Butler landed at Bermuda Hundred, a bottle-shaped piece of land made by a bend in the James. This he fortified and made the base of his operations. But the Confederates under Beauregard defeated him at Drury's Bluff, and forcing him within his de-

R. E. Lee

fenses imprisoned him by building a line of strong fortifications across the neck of his bottle, thus for the time
rendering him harmless. General Grant said that "his
army was as completely shut off as if it had been in a
bottle strongly corked."

Defeat of Sigel at New Market. — Early in May, General
Sigel with seven thousand men advanced up the Valley;

Cadets at New Market

but at New Market, General John C. Breckenridge defeated him and forced him to retreat. Just before the
battle, a battalion of cadets from the Virginia Military
Institute, two hundred and thirty strong, came under the
command of Colonel Ship to aid the Confederates in driving Sigel back, and in the engagement behaved with distinguished gallantry. The cadets occupied a position in
the Confederate line just in front of Sigel's artillery bat-
tery, which they charged with the steadiness of old veterans

and captured, bayoneting some of the cannoneers who
stood to their guns. When the battle was over, forty-six
of the brave boys lay upon the field wounded and eight
were dead. This incident shows that even the boys were
filled with the determination to fight the war out to its
bitter end.

Early defeats Hunter and threatens Washington. — On
the first of June, 1864, General David Hunter, who after
the battle of New Market had succeeded Sigel, was commanded by the Federal authorities to begin another campaign in the Valley, the special object of which was to
capture Lynchburg. Near Port Republic he defeated
General W. E. Jones, whom General Lee had ordered from
southwest Virginia to defend the Valley. After doing this
he was reënforced by cavalry under Generals Crook and
Averill, which raised his force to eighteen thousand, and
now for a time he went his way without serious opposition.
His march was marked by the most wanton destruction of
property. At Lexington he burned the Virginia Military
Institute, the residence of Governor Letcher, and other
private property. On reaching Lynchburg he encountered General Early,[1] whom Lee, after defeating Grant at
Cold Harbor, had sent with a detachment of troops to defend the city. Hunter now retreated precipitately towards
West Virginia. In July, Early marched into Maryland,
and, though he had but twelve thousand men, he approached within cannon shot of Washington, but found
the city too strongly garrisoned to venture to attack it
with his small force. Later he made a raid into Pennsyl-

[1] Jubal A. Early was born in Virginia in 1818, graduated at West Point,
and served in the Mexican War, rising to the rank of colonel. He was among
the first to volunteer in the service of the Confederacy. After the war he
engaged in the practice of law. He died in Lynchburg in 1894.

vania and burned Chambersburg in retaliation for Hunter's vandalism in the Valley.

Sheridan's Devastation of the Valley. — Early's operations in the Valley proved so troublesome to the Federals that, in August, General Grant sent Sheridan with forty thousand men to dislodge him. After much maneuvering, Sheridan finally defeated Early, and then by Grant's orders he laid the Valley waste, killing cattle and sheep, carrying off horses, and burning barns, mills, farming implements, grain, and hay. The work of destruction was so complete in this most fertile part of Virginia, that Sheridan, it is said, asserted that "a crow, flying across the Valley, must carry its own rations."

Siege of Petersburg. — Grant crossed the James the middle of June and hoped to capture Petersburg before Lee's army could come to its defense. But in this he was disappointed. The first assaults that were made were repulsed by Beauregard's troops, who succeeded in holding the city for three days; and then the torn battle-flags of the Army of Northern Virginia were seen floating above the hastily constructed fortifications. Lee's army had arrived. On the very day that Lee's veterans reached Petersburg, Grant made two desperate attempts to take the Confederate works by storm; but his troops were driven back with a loss of nine thousand. Lee continued to improve the defenses of the city till they were impregnable from assault. A separate chain of fortifications provided for the defense of Richmond; but General Grant's main efforts were directed against Petersburg, as a capture of this city would lead to the fall of Richmond.

Battle of the Crater. — The first attempts to capture Petersburg having ended in failure, Grant now tried to get possession of the beleaguered city by a novel ex-

pedient. Burnside's Ninth Corps lay intrenched within
one hundred and fifty yards of an angle in the Confederate works, which was covered by a fort. Under this
point General Grant, at a suggestion of Burnside, had a
mine dug in which was stored eighty hundredweight of gunpowder. On July 30 the mine was exploded, blowing the
fort and its garrison of two hundred and fifty-six men high

Battle of the Crater

into the air, and leaving a crater thirty feet deep, sixty feet
wide, and one hundred and seventy feet long. The Federal
batteries at once opened on the Confederate works, while
an assaulting column moved up to storm them. But the
Confederates speedily regained their self-possession, and
turned their guns upon the besiegers, who, having rushed
through the opening, found themselves enfiladed from the
right and the left by artillery and fusilladed from the front

by musketry. The end came when Lee sent General Mahone with two brigades of Hill's corps, who drove the stormers back and retook the whole line. The crater was for the Federals a hideous slaughter pen. Their loss was four thousand, and Grant said the affair was a "stupendous failure."

Situation at the End of 1864. — In November, 1864, President Lincoln was elected for a second term, which showed that the North intended to continue to carry on the war vigorously. By the end of the year, the power of the Confederacy in the West had been almost entirely destroyed. The eleven states she started with had been practically reduced to three — Virginia, North Carolina, and South Carolina. Sherman had marched through Georgia, and was preparing to cross the Carolinas and enter Virginia with an army of sixty thousand men. Lee, it is true, had defeated Grant again and again; but his victories had been fruitless; for he had not been able, with the slender resources at his command, to destroy the Federal army, nor to drive it out of Virginia. The Confederacy had about come to the end of her resources. Her money was nearly worthless,[1] and her credit was gone. The brave men that had fallen in battle she could not replace. The soldiers that remained in her armies were veterans that could be relied on; but they were opposed by four times as many men on the Federal side. The course of events

[1] Toward the end of the Confederacy, the currency had depreciated to such an extent that when a man went to market, it was said, he carried his money in a basket and brought what he purchased back in his pocket. In 1865, flour was $1000 per barrel, coffee $50 to $60 per pound, black pepper $300 per pound, and other things in proportion. For tea raspberry leaves and sassafras roots were used, and for sugar sorghum was substituted. In 1864, a coat and vest of coarse homespun cost $250, and a lady's dress which was worth before the war only $10, could not be purchased for less than $500.

had been such as to indicate the speedy collapse of the Confederacy from exhaustion; but neither the South nor the North realized how near this was at hand, so wonderful had been the defensive warfare waged by General Lee.

QUESTIONS

1. Describe the raid of Kilpatrick and Dahlgren.
2. Who was Ulysses S. Grant, and for what was he noted?
3. What was Grant's " Hammering Campaign "?
4. Describe the battles of the Wilderness. Give relative strength of the two armies.
5. What occurred at Cold Harbor?
6. What is said of Lee's generalship?
7. How did Beauregard render Butler harmless?
8. What did Grant say of Butler's army?
9. Describe the gallant conduct of the cadets of the Virginia Military Institute, at New Market.
10. Describe Hunter's campaign in the Valley.
11. What vandalism did he commit at Lexington?
12. By whom was he met, and defeated?
13. Why did not Early continue his march, and attack Washington?
14. Whom did Grant send to defeat Early, and with how many men?
15. What did Sheridan do in the Valley, and what assertion did he make ?
16. What did Grant hope to do on crossing the James?
17. How were his first assaults repulsed?
18. Give an account of the Petersburg mine.
19. How did it recoil upon the Federals?
20. What did Grant say of it?
21. What did the reëlection of Lincoln show the South?
22. To what limits had the Confederacy been reduced at the end of 1864?
23. What was Sherman now preparing to do?
24. What is said of the resources of the Confederacy?

CHAPTER XXVIII

END OF THE WAR

Evacuation of Richmond and Petersburg. — During the autumn and winter (1864-'65) General Grant fortified his position; and, while his cavalry laid waste the country that furnished supplies to the Confederates, his infantry gradually extended their lines westward, till Lee was forced to guard fortifications thirty-five or forty miles in length. To do this, in March, 1865, he had about forty thousand half-starved and half-clothed men, while in front of him lay Grant's well-equipped army of three or four times that number. Grant received a continual stream of reënforcements to make good any losses he might sustain. Lee could get none. The crisis came in the spring of 1865. On April 2, Grant pierced Lee's thin lines in several places, and thus rendered the evacuation [1] of Richmond and Petersburg

---

[1] Strange to say, the people of Richmond had no idea that the city was about to be evacuated. This is accounted for by the fact that for some time the newspapers had been warned by the Confederate government not to publish any news except such as the War Department gave out. The impression prevailed that General Johnston was going to unite his army with Lee's, and that then an offensive movement would be made against the Federals. But this fancied security came suddenly to an end. On the morning of April 2, while President Davis was attending service at St. Paul's church, a messenger brought him a dispatch from General Lee which announced that the Confederate lines had been broken, and that unless they could be reëstablished, when night came the city would have to be evacuated. Davis maintained his composure, but immediately left the church. Soon the rumor was heard on the streets that the time had come when Lee could no longer hold the beleaguered city, and by the afternoon even the most incredulous saw unmistakable signs that the evacuation was at hand.

230

necessary. On the night of the 2nd, General Lee withdrew his troops from the fortifications they had so long and so gallantly defended, and began to retreat toward Danville, his plan being to reach North Carolina and unite his army with that of General Joseph E. Johnston.

The Conflagration in Richmond. — On the morning of April 3 the Federals took possession of Richmond, which they found to be on fire, the conflagration having its origin in the burning of some public buildings by the Confederates as they retreated. The city presented a scene of the wildest confusion. Bands of men were plundering the stores, while the streets were full of homeless people, whose cries of distress were heard on all sides. Nearly one third of the city was laid in ruins before the progress of the flames could be arrested, but this was finally done by the combined efforts of the citizens and Federal authorities.

Surrender of General Lee. — Lee had ordered rations to be sent to Amelia Courthouse for his army ; but, owing to some mistake, this was not done. His forces reached this point on April 4. They were without food, and in endeavoring to get provisions from the country they lost nearly twenty-four hours. On the evening of April 4th, Sheridan's cavalry reached Jetersville on the Richmond and Danville railroad, which caused Lee, when he resumed his retreat, to leave the line of the railroad and turn toward Lynchburg. When he reached Appomattox Courthouse, he found Sheridan's cavalry in his front and also an infantry line of battle, while the main body of the Army of the Potomac was in his rear. His forces were surrounded, and he realized that further resistance would but lead to the sacrifice of the remnant of the brave army, which under his leadership had proved itself invincible on so many hard-

fought fields. Accordingly on the 9th of April he surrendered to General Grant the shattered remnant of his
noble army, numbering about twenty-eight thousand men,
but of these only eight thousand bore arms.

Grant's Generous Spirit. — General Grant in this hour of
triumph showed no disposition to exult over his great
antagonist. Instead of this he treated him with the most

Arlington, Lee's Home

delicate consideration. He did not demand Lee's sword,
and it was not offered to him. He only required that the
men should lay down their arms. Those that had horses
were allowed to retain them. "They will need them for
their spring plowing," General Grant said.

General Lee taking Leave of his Army. — It was a sad
sight when General Lee took leave of his army. His soldiers crowded up to him, anxious to touch him, or even his
horse. In bidding them farewell their great commander

said: "Men, we have fought through the war together; I have done my best for you; my heart is too full to say more."

Downfall of the Confederacy. — The surrender of Lee was followed by that of General Joseph E. Johnston to General Sherman, which took place in North Carolina on April 26. Then in rapid succession the Confederate armies in other parts of the South laid down their arms. The South was fighting for independence, and the overthrow of the Army of Northern Virginia convinced her that she could not succeed. When this became evident, the Confederacy went down at once; and the great contest came to a sudden end.

No Trials of Confederate Leaders. — President Davis was captured on May 10, in Georgia, and imprisoned in Fortress Monroe. Mr. Stanton, Secretary of State under President Lincoln, endeavored to bring the illustrious captive to trial for cruelty to Federal prisoners, who had suffered at Andersonville for supplies which the South was unable to give them; but in this effort he failed. For two years, however, Jefferson Davis remained a prisoner, and was then released on bail; but neither he nor any other Confederate leader was ever tried for taking part in the secession movement.

Supremacy of the Nation. — The war accomplished the object for which the North fought — the restoration of the Union. The result proved that a majority of the citizens of the United States had decided that the Union should be a nation and not a confederacy of sovereign states as it was when the Constitution was adopted. No amendment embodying this was made to the Constitution; but the right of secession had been submitted to the arbitrament of arms and the decision had been that it must be given up, and thus the supremacy of the nation was established.

Abolition of Slavery. — The course of events was also such as to bring about the abolition of slavery.[1] President Lincoln, in 1863, issued an emancipation proclamation as a war measure to help bring about the defeat of the South; and while this was immediately effective only in territory occupied by the Federals, yet once published, it was never recalled; for, as time passed, it became a settled conviction all through the North and the West that slavery should not survive the war. Accordingly, after the struggle was over, amendments, which gave the negro his freedom, made him a citizen, and secured to him his rights, were made to the Constitution.

The Army of Northern Virginia. — The rank and file of the Army of Northern Virginia was made up largely of gentlemen of birth, fortune, and education. In the Rockbridge artillery there were twenty-eight college graduates, and in a company of infantry that went from the Northern Neck of Virginia, there were sixteen graduates of the Virginia Military Institute. The heroic deeds of the army were due to the fact that each private soldier, whether rich or poor, of high or low estate, felt that he was fighting for a principle, and so each one entered into the contest with the spirit that animated the European noblesse in the wars of the Middle Ages.

[1] At first the people of the North fought to preserve the Union with slavery; but, after January 1, 1863, when President Lincoln issued the Emancipation Proclamation, their object was to preserve the Union and abolish slavery. To preserve the Union was the aim which President Lincoln set before himself. Early in the war he said: "If the Union can best be saved by emancipating all the slaves, I am willing to emancipate them all; if it can best be saved by emancipating part, I am ready to emancipate a part; and if it can best be *saved by not* emancipating any, I will emancipate none."

A Northern Tribute to Virginia. — During the war the *Washington Republican*, an organ that advocated the abolition of slavery, published the following handsome tribute to Virginia: "If there has been any decadence of the manly virtues in the Old Dominion, it is not because the present generation has proved itself either weak or cowardly or unequal to the greatest emergencies. No people with so few numbers ever put into the field, and kept there so long, troops more numerous, brave, or more efficient, or produced generals of more merit in all kinds and grades of military talent.[1] It is not a worn-out and effete race that has produced Lee, Johnston, Jackson, Ashby,[2] and Stuart. It is not a worn-out and effete race

---

[1] Dr. Hunter McGuire, Medical Director Second Army Corps (Stonewall Jackson's), Army of Northern Virginia, in a lecture on Stonewall Jackson, says: "It was with a swelling heart that I recently heard some of the first soldiers and military students of England declare that within the past two hundred years the English-speaking race had produced but five soldiers of the first rank — Marlborough, Washington, Wellington, Robert E. Lee, and Stonewall Jackson. I heard them declare that Jackson's campaign in the Shenandoah Valley was the finest specimen of strategy and tactics of which the world has any record; that in this series of marches and battles there was never a blunder, and that this campaign was superior to either of those made by Napoleon in Italy. One British officer who teaches strategy in a great European college told me that he used this campaign as a model, and dwelt upon it for months in his lectures, and that it was taught in all military schools of Germany, and Von Molke declared it was without a rival in the world's history. 'Indeed,' he added, 'Jackson seems to me to have been inspired.' Another British soldier of high rank and a trained student of war told me that for its numbers the Army of Northern Virginia had more force and power than any other army that ever existed."

[2] Turner Ashby was born at Rosehill, Fauquier Co, Va., in 1824. He was appointed a brigadier general in 1862, and was distinguished as a cavalry leader. Of him, Jackson wrote: "As a partisan officer, I never knew his superior. His daring was proverbial, his powers of endurance almost incredible, his tone of character heroic, and his sagacity almost intuitive in divining the purposes and movements of the enemy." To defend Virginia was the one

which for two years has defended its capital against the approach of an enemy close upon their borders and outnumbering them thirty to one. It is not a worn-out and effete race which has preserved substantial popular unity under all the straits and pressure and sacrifice of this unprecedented war."

QUESTIONS

1. What did Grant do in the autumn and winter of 1865?
2. What was the condition of Lee's army at this time, and what were its numbers?
3. Give the steps that led to the evacuation of Richmond and Petersburg.
4. Describe the conflagration in Richmond.
5. Give an account of the surrender of Lee. When did it take place?
6. What was the respective strength of the two armies at the time?
7. How did Grant show a generous spirit?
8. Describe Lee's farewell to his army.
9. What followed Lee's surrender?
10. When and where was President Davis imprisoned?
11. Was he or any other Confederate leader ever tried?
12. What did the war establish in regard to the nation?
13. Why had Lincoln issued the Emancipation Proclamation in 1863?
14. After the war, what amendments were made to the Constitution?
15. What was the character of the men that composed the Army of Northern Virginia?
16. Give the tribute paid to Virginia by the *Washington Republican*.
17. What do European critics say of Jackson's Valley Campaign and the Army of Northern Virginia?
18. Who was Turner Ashby, and what is said of him?

thought that filled Ashby's heart. At Harper's Ferry, just as the war opened, some one asked him under what banner he was going to fight. He took from his hat a small flag of Virginia, and pointing to it said, "That is the flag I intend to fight under." On the 6th of June, 1862, in a sharp skirmish near Harrisonburg, the gallant Turner Ashby, the famous "Knight of the Valley," was struck by a minie ball and killed instantly.

REVIEW QUESTIONS

1. Describe the battle of Chancellorsville.
2. Give an account of the death of Stonewall Jackson.
3. Describe the cavalry battle of Brandy Station.
4. Tell of the battle of Gettysburg, and what is said of this battle.
5. What plan did Grant form for subjugating the South?
6. Describe the battles of the Wilderness.
7. What is said of Lee's generalship?
8. Describe Butler's imprisonment.
9. Tell of the bravery of the cadets at New Market.
10. Give an account of Hunter's march through the Valley, and Early's defeat of him.
11. Of Sheridan's devastation of the Valley.
12. Describe the siege of Petersburg.
13. The battle of the Crater.
14. What was the situation at the end of 1864?
15. Tell of the evacuation of Richmond and Petersburg.
16. When and where did General Lee surrender, and what was the respective numbers of the two armies?
17. What is said of Grant's generous spirit?
18. Give Lee's farewell words to his army.
19. Tell about the downfall of the Confederacy, and the results of the war.
20. Describe the Army of Northern Virginia, and give the tribute paid to the state by a Northern paper.

CHAPTER XXIX

Condition of Virginia after the War. — Virginia had poured out her resources in a lavish stream to meet the ever-increasing needs of the Confederate government. She had borne the brunt of the war; and great was the devastation brought upon her by the conflict through which she had passed. When the end came, her condition was deplorable. Her slaves had been forcibly freed, and, all over her territory, houses had been burned, fences destroyed, cattle killed, and farms devastated. Worse than all this, her fields had been drenched with blood; and the land was filled with mourning for fathers, brothers, husbands, and sons, who had gone forth to battle and had never returned.

Suspension of Civil Government. — When Richmond was evacuated, the state government, as it existed under the Confederacy, came practically to an end. Governor Smith, it is true, moved the seat of the government to Lynchburg; but, becoming convinced after the surrender of General Lee that any further effort on the part of the state to continue the war would be useless, he gave himself up to the Federal authorities and received ·his parole.

On April 6 President Lincoln issued an order which authorized the legislature to assemble at Richmond, but this he recalled[1] before a formal meeting of the body was held.

[1] General Grant lays the responsibility of the recall of the permission for the meeting of the legislature of Virginia entirely upon Secretary Stanton. See Grant's *Memoirs*, Vol. II., p. 506.

Provisional Government Established. — Unfortunately for Virginia, President Lincoln was assassinated[1] by John Wilkes Booth soon after the evacuation of Richmond. Had Lincoln lived, the people believed that the state would have been speedily restored to her place in the Union, and this his successor, President Johnson, tried to bring about, but he was unable to control the dominant party in Congress. One month after Lee's surrender, Johnson, in following out his plan for the restoration of the state, appointed Francis H. Pierpont provisional governor.

Refused Readmission into the Union. — Governor Pierpont,[2] in taking charge of affairs, showed a patriotic

[1] On the night of April 14, President Lincoln, with his wife and some friends, was seated in a box at Ford's theater, Washington, D. C., when Booth crept in and shot him with a pistol. The wounded President was carried to a house near the theater, and all that medical skill could suggest was done for him. But the bullet had penetrated his brain, and he died the next morning. Booth, after firing the fatal shot, leaped from the box, but his spur caught in an American flag, and he fell heavily, breaking his leg. Such wild confusion prevailed, however, that he made his escape from the building, and mounting a horse held in readiness for him by an accomplice, rode rapidly away. But he was pursued, and finally found in an old barn near Bowling Green, Va. As he refused to surrender, the building was set on fire, and he was shot.

[2] Mr. Pierpont had been, since January 1, 1864, governor of what was known as "Restored Virginia," the history of which was as follows: After West Virginia became a separate state, the Union people living in ten counties and parts of counties organized at Alexandria a government loyal to the United States, and elected Pierpont governor. This "restored government" was a feeble organization, its General Assembly never numbering, it is said, more than sixteen. Under its auspices, however, a convention was called which adopted an amended constitution, one clause of which provided for the abolition of slavery. President Johnson, in the proclamation he issued on May 9, 1865, recognized the "restored government" as the true and lawful one for Virginia. Pierpont then transferred his seat of government from Alexandria to Richmond, and on June 20, 1865, called a special session of his legislature. The elections that took place in October, 1865, were held under the authority of the "restored government."

spirit in his efforts to reëstablish the state government. On October 12, 1865, elections were held for members of the General Assembly and of Congress. But when the representatives of Virginia appeared in Washington, Congress refused to allow them to take their seats, and, before its adjournment, decided not to readmit into the Union any state that had formed a part of the Confederacy, till it would ratify the fourteenth amendment to the Federal Constitution. This made the negro a citizen and put the political and military leaders of the Confederacy under disability to hold office. Virginia refused to take the action required of her, and so was not readmitted. Governor Pierpont continued to administer the provisional government established by President Johnson, and the people displayed a law-abiding spirit. The state government was theoretically independent, but the military authorities frequently interfered with the operations of the civil law.

Under Military Rule. — Finally, in 1867, Congress passed over the President's veto the Reconstruction Acts, which put Virginia under military rule. By these measures the government existing in the state was made entirely subordinate to a military commander, who had authority to administer all the powers of the state, life and liberty being subject to such military commissions as he might create. The courts of the state could sit, but only by permission of the commander. During this period no one was allowed to vote or hold office unless he could take an oath [1] that he

[1] This was known as the ironclad oath, which was as follows: " I . . . do solemnly swear that I have never voluntarily borne arms against the United States since I have been a citizen thereof; that I have voluntarily given no aid, countenance, counsel, or encouragement to persons engaged in armed hostility thereto; that I have never sought, nor accepted, nor attempted to exercise the functions of any office whatever, under any authority or pretended authority in hostility to the United States; that I have not yielded a voluntary

had never borne arms against the United States, and had never given aid to the Confederacy, nor held an office under its authority.

The Rule of " Carpet-baggers " [1] **and " Scallawags "** [2]. — Under the test oath required but few white men could take part in politics, and so the government of the state fell into the hands of "Carpet-baggers," "Scallawags," and negroes. For a time there was a reign of ignorance, fraud, and robbery, during which the state debt, already a very heavy one, was increased over thirteen millions. Two of the military commanders complained to the authorities at Washington that it was impossible, under the test oath required, to find enough competent persons to fill the offices in the state.

In the Union again. — In 1870 the state was readmitted into the Union under a constitution which accepted all the legislation that had been made in regard to the negro, but without any clause disfranchising the citizens who had taken part in the War of Secession. After this the government came into the hands of those competent to administer it, and soon law and order prevailed throughout the commonwealth. President Grant aided in rescuing the state from the rule of the " Carpet-baggers " and " Scallawags," by using his influence in getting the disfranchising clause submitted to a separate vote which resulted in its rejection.

support to any pretended government, authority, power, or constitution within the United States, hostile or inimical thereto; and . . . that . . . I will support and defend the constitution of the United States against all enemies . . .'' etc.

[1] A Northern politician who, possessing nothing but a carpet-bag came South to get plunder and office, was called by the people a " Carpet-bagger."

[2] The few renegade Southerners, who joined with the " Carpet-baggers " in their plundering schemes, were denominated in derision " Scallawags."

The Freedmen's Bureau. — An account of the Reconstruction period would be incomplete without a notice of
the Freedmen's Bureau. As the war drew to an end, the
number of negroes dependent upon the Federal government had become so great that Congress established in
connection with the War Department a bureau, which was
to have control of all matters relating to refugees and
freedmen from the territory that had been in the Confederacy. It was authorized to issue provisions, clothing,
fuel, and medical supplies to the destitute. It had power
also to take charge of abandoned or confiscated land, and
to rent it to refugees and freedmen in forty-acre tracts for
a term of three years. At the end of this time, the bureau
could sell the land to the occupants. This provision gave
rise to a widespread belief among the negroes that it was
the purpose of the government to give each one of them
"forty acres and a mule." The hope of this expected
legacy, which was for a long time cherished, had the effect
of increasing idleness. It was used, too, by unscrupulous
adventurers from the North to extort money from the
negroes, on the promise that the land would be divided
out among them as soon as they all paid a small fee.

The establishment of the Freedmen's Bureau was due
to sectional prejudice, which ran high in 1865, and to a
mistaken idea that it would prove a benefit to the negro
race. In Virginia and elsewhere its operations ended in
failure.

Wreck of the Plantation System. — The plantation system
that had existed from the earliest period came to a sudden
end with Lee's surrender. After this event, the conditions
of country life were practically revolutionized. The obliga-
tion that had rested upon a master to feed, clothe, take
care of, and protect his slaves for life-time services was

changed at once to a business contract between master and servant, which could be easily terminated. For a short time, in most parts of the state, the negroes remained upon the land of their former masters. Then the desire to enjoy their newly acquired freedom caused them to move from place to place, and to seek busy centers. Soon the deserted and roofless cabins that were seen all over the country were unmistakable and melancholy signs that the plantation system, as it existed in the olden times, was no more.

Spirit of the People. — The Virginians have always been known as a sanguine people; and this phase of their character came out prominently in the way they accepted the issues of the war without repining. They addressed themselves resolutely to the difficult task of restoring their ruined homes, when they were without capital, without credit, and in many cases hopelessly involved in debt. Men, who had never done a day's work in their lives but had lived in comfort upon the labor of their slaves, began at once to cultivate the land with their own hands; and fair women, brought up in luxury and accustomed to all the refinements of life, performed without a murmur household drudgery, to which they had been strangers. The heroic spirit the people had displayed when tried in the fiery ordeal of war was not more admirable than the patient endurance and self-control they manifested in adjusting themselves to the new conditions that confronted them.

QUESTIONS

1. Describe the condition of Virginia after the Civil War.
2. What is said of the suspension of civil government?
3. Give an account of President Lincoln's assassination.
4. What did President Johnson wish to do for the state, and what kind of governor did he appoint?

5. Give the history of "Restored Virginia."
6. What happened when Virginia's representatives appeared in Washington?
7. Why was she refused readmission into the Union?
8. Describe the military rule under which the state was put by Congress.
9. Who were the "Carpet-baggers" and "Scallawags"?
10. What was the ironclad oath?
11. When and under what conditions did Virginia enter the Union again?
12. What was the Freedmen's Bureau?
13. How did it prove an injury to the negro?
14. When and in what way was the plantation system wrecked?
15. Describe the spirit of the people in adjusting themselves to the changed condition of affairs.

CHAPTER XXX

READJUSTMENT

Capitol Disaster. — A few months after the civil government of Virginia had been restored, an unexpected catastrophe spread sorrow throughout the state. A great crowd had assembled in the chamber of the Court of Appeals to hear a decision which would determine whether Ellyson, who had been elected mayor of Richmond, had a right to the office, or Chahoon, who had been appointed under the military authorities. While the people were waiting for the verdict, which was in favor of Mayor Ellyson, the floor gave way, and the crowd was precipitated into the legislative hall below. Sixty-five persons were killed and more than two hundred sustained injuries. A number of the most prominent citizens were among the killed and wounded.

Last Days of General Lee. — General Lee spent his last days in Virginia, which he loved so well. After the war was over he believed that it was the duty of all who wished to take part in the restoration of their state to render allegiance to the Federal government; and so he applied to President Johnson for amnesty under the terms of the proclamation issued by him. His example kept many Virginians from hastily abandoning their state in the hour of defeat. In the autumn of 1865 Lee accepted the presidency of Washington College, where for the remainder of his life he devoted himself as conscientiously to the work of education, as he had formerly done to the prosecution of the war. He died in 1870, at the age of sixty-three. His ability, with the high and noble virtues of his character, mark him as one of the greatest Americans that the nineteenth century has produced. Lord Wolseley says he has met but two men who filled his ideal of what a true hero should be, and one of these was Robert E. Lee.

Public School System. — Virginia has had much to contend with in regard to public schools. In colonial days education was not encouraged except among the higher classes, Governor Berkeley going so far as to say: "I thank God there are no free schools nor printing, and I hope we shall not have these hundred years; for learning has brought disobedience and heresy and sects into the world, and printing has divulged them, and libels against the best government. God keep us from both." After the Revolution much interest was manifested by Thomas Jefferson and others in public education. No provision, however, for schools, supported by the state, for the education of all the people was made till 1870 when the present public school system went into operation. When the schools were first opened, the money supplied by the state for their support was insufficient and there was a good deal of opposition to them coming from people who did not for various reasons believe in public education. So Dr. William H. Ruffner, who was elected by the legislature the first superintendent of public instruction, met with many difficulties in organizing the system. He labored faithfully to put the schools on a good foundation, and accomplished much in spite of lack of funds and the prejudice that existed against his work.[1] He served as

[1] William H. Ruffner was born in 1824 at Lexington, Va. He was educated at Washington College, where he took the degree of A.M. He then

superintendent twelve years, and lived long enough after his retirement to see his pioneer work bear good fruit in the hands of his successors.

The White House of the Confederacy. — The mansion in Richmond formerly occupied by President Davis, and

The White House of the Confederacy (Confederate Museum)

known as the White House of the Confederacy, is now a museum for the preservation of Confederate relics, and also

studied at the Union Theological Seminary and at Princeton. Entering the ministry of the Presbyterian Church, he served two years as chaplain at the University of Virginia, and after this was pastor of a church in Philadelphia. In 1853 he retired from the ministry on account of ill health, and engaged in farming. In 1870, when the public school system was established in Virginia, he was elected first superintendent of public instruction. In 1884 he was elected first president of the State Female Normal School at Farmville, Va. He died at Lexington, Va., in 1908.

the repository of the records of the Southern Historical Society. Each state that belonged to the Confederacy has a separate room in which it places its valued relics. In the Virginia room are to be found memorials of Lee, Jackson, Johnston, Pickett, Stuart, A. P. Hill, and of other illustrious sons too numerous to be mentioned here. Among the documents preserved in the building by the Southern Historical Society, are valued autograph letters of the leading Confederate generals and the copy of the " Paroles of the Army of Northern Virginia " that was made out for General Lee. This museum of Confederate relics is not designed either to arouse or to keep alive sectional feeling, but to perpetuate the deeds, the hardships, and the self-denial of a patriotic people. Virginia is thoroughly loyal to the restored Union, but at the same time she is true to her past and cherishes tenderly the memory of the Confederacy.[1]

Patriotic Societies. — Such patriotic societies as the " Colonial Dames," " Daughters of the American Revolution," and " United Daughters of the Confederacy " are enthusiastically sustained by Virginia women, who thus in times of peace keep alive in the memory of the people the deeds of their forefathers. Though Virginia is the oldest settlement of English people outside of England, she for a long time did but little toward saving from destruction relics of her early history. But the women of the state became interested in the matter and in 1889 formed an

[1] The Confederate Memorial Institute, popularly called the " Battle Abbey," is located in Richmond. This impressive building was erected to perpetuate the memory of those distinguished in the civil and military life of the Confederacy and to preserve the relics of that heroic period. The cornerstone was laid in 1912, and the building was opened to the public for the first time during the Confederate reunion in 1915, though it was not at that time completed in all its appointments.

Association for the Preservation of Virginia Antiquities, which is doing much valuable work.

Patriotism of Virginia Women.[1]— No history of Virginia which does not chronicle the influence women have exerted in shaping the destiny of the state would be complete. During the uncertain years of the Revolution and also in the trying days of the Civil War, they sent their loved ones to battle for their country with the same heroic spirit that animated the Spartan mother when she bade her son farewell with the injunction, " Come back with your shield or upon it." Nor did they remain inactive at home, but ministered to the sick and wounded with the most unremitting care, taking charge of hospitals and sustaining them largely by their own contributions. At the same time they encouraged those who were bearing arms in the field, and rendered them aid in every way that ingenuity could devise. When all this is taken into consideration, it is evident that they deserve a share in the state's heroic achievements as truly as do the most valiant soldiers.

Yorktown Centennial. — The hundredth anniversary of the surrender of Cornwallis was celebrated at Yorktown in 1881, and the occasion brought to Virginia visitors from all over the country and from Europe. The United States sent a large number of soldiers to Yorktown ; and her war ships gathered in the neighborhood, while from Europe came representatives of France and Germany and descendants of the foreign officers who were with the Americans when the surrender took place. The celebration lasted for six days, and was characterized by military and naval reviews, which were witnessed by thousands of the inhabitants of the state.

[1] A handsome memorial tablet to the Confederate Women of Virginia was unveiled in Hollywood Cemetery in 1915 during the Confederate reunion.

The State Debt — its Origin. — Virginia realized soon after the Revolution that she could not get her great resources developed without means of transportation. So between 1784 and 1861, she borrowed money to make her rivers deeper in order that they could be navigated,[1] and to construct canals, turnpikes, and railroads.[2] She obtained this money from parties in the Northern states and in Europe, and gave them her bonds for it at six per cent interest. She did not try to carry on these works of "internal improvement," as they were called, by herself, but became a partner in companies that undertook to construct them, by investing the money she had borrowed in the stock of these companies. In this way the state borrowed a very large sum of money.[3]

The Debt in 1861. — The debt was, in 1861, more than thirty million dollars. Little or no interest was paid during the Civil War and the Reconstruction period, and so in 1871 the debt together with the unpaid interest amounted to about forty-seven million dollars. One third of this amount was assigned by the Virginia legislature to West Virginia, as she had been formed into a separate state and had thus taken away about one third of the territory and population of the original state of Virginia. The legislature passed a law authorizing new bonds, bearing six per

---

[1] The first company formed to improve rivers was the James River Company, which in 1784 secured a charter from the legislature to deepen the James from Richmond to Botetourt County. A number of other companies for the improvement of rivers were chartered later.

[2] The first railroad company was chartered in 1830 to build a railroad from Petersburg, Va., to Weldon, N. C.

[3] The need of large sums of money is shown by the fact that from 1784 to 1861, Virginia aided in building 122 turnpikes, 12 canals, and 20 railroads. In addition to this, she helped construct a great many bridges and aided in *improving most* of the important rivers.

cent interest, to be issued to the creditors of the state for the amount due them with interest after taking off West Virginia's part.

Rise of the Readjuster Party. — A serious difficulty was met with in carrying out this law. The debt remaining to Virginia, without counting West Virginia's part, was so large, and the state so impoverished as the result of war, that her revenues did not prove to be large enough, though taxes were high, to pay the interest on her debt and meet the expenses of government. So the debt question became a very live issue, and there was much discussion in regard to it. The outlook for the state seemed dark. Under the leadership of General William Mahone, a noted Confederate officer, there now rose a party which held ·that the state was trying to pay too much, and that the debt ought to be "readjusted" and a lower rate of interest paid. This party soon made itself strongly felt.

Another Law Passed. — As a result of the continual agitation of the debt question, the legislature in 1879 passed a new law, known as the McCulloch law, by the terms of which the state agreed still to give bonds for all the debt, but at a lower rate of interest.

Triumph of the Readjusters. — Though this new law lowered the interest on the state debt, which was one thing the Readjusters demanded, it did not satisfy them. So they proceeded at once to marshal their forces in order to change it. Their party now grew very rapidly, finally drawing into its ranks most of the Republicans and many Democrats.[1] No hotter political campaign ever took place in Virginia than that waged over the settlement of the state debt. The final contest between the opposing forces

[1] During this period the Democratic party was called the Conservative party.

came in November, 1881, and resulted in a complete triumph for the Readjusters, who elected the governor and a majority in both branches of the legislature. The Readjusters, being now in full power, passed a law in 1882 to the effect that the state would not pay on the debt any interest that had accumulated before that date. This was known as the Riddleberger law. By taking off all the back interest, the debt was now reduced to about twenty-one millions, and provision was made for issuing bonds bearing three per cent interest for this amount. This was called "readjusting" the state debt, and the party that did this was known as the Readjuster party.

End of the Readjuster Party. — The Democratic party, finding itself hopelessly in the minority, agreed to accept the Readjuster legislation in regard to the debt in order again to get control of the state government. Then the Readjuster party, having accomplished its object, began to fall to pieces and soon ceased to exist. Most of the Democrats who had followed Mahone returned to the regular Democratic party, though some of them went to the Republicans, General Mahone being among the number. The Republicans who had arrayed themselves under the Readjuster standard returned to their party. These changes took place rapidly. In the elections of November, 1883, the Democrats carried both branches of the legislature, and with the election of General Fitzhugh Lee as governor in 1885 again came into full control of the state government.

Settlement with the Bondholders. — The creditors were not disposed to accept the settlement of the debt made by the Readjusters, and greatly annoyed the state with lawsuits. Happily, however, in 1892 they entered into an agreement with the legislature by which their claims were *finally settled.*

Controversy with West Virginia. — West Virginia refused to pay the part of the debt owed by the original
state of Virginia that had been assigned to her, and this
led to a long controversy. Virginia finally brought suit in
the United States Supreme Court to make West Virginia
pay. The case was argued in 1908, and in 1911 the court
decided that West Virginia should pay a part of the debt
that existed at the beginning of 1861, as she was at that
time a part of Old Virginia. The court fixed West Virginia's share at about seven million dollars, and left the
question of interest to be disposed of by the two states.
West Virginia refused to pay this amount,[1] and in 1914
succeeded in getting the matter reopened in the Supreme
Court on the ground that new evidence had been discovered. In June, 1915, the court rendered its final decision,
which was that West Virginia should pay her part of the
old debt, both principal and interest. This was fixed at
about twelve and one third million dollars.[1] Thus the
long contest ended in victory for Virginia.

Virginia at the World's Fair. — At the great Columbian
Exposition held in Chicago in 1893 to commemorate the
four hundredth anniversary of the discovery of America,
the Virginia exhibit was displayed in a building which was
an exact representation of the home of Washington at
Mount Vernon, and contained much of the furniture of
that historic structure. It was filled with a rare collection
of relics of the Colonial and Revolutionary periods. The

---

[1] The amounts in regard to the state debt are given in round numbers.
The exact figures are as follows:

Debt of Old Virginia at the beginning of 1861 . $30,563,861.56
Amount the court decided in 1911 that West Vir-
ginia should pay . . . . 7,182,507.46 and interest
Total amount fixed by the court in 1915 for West
Virginia to pay 12,393,929.50

novelty of the building and interesting character of its contents caused it to attract greater attention than many others that were far more costly and magnificent.

Fire at the University of Virginia. — On October 27, 1895, a fire broke out in the Public Hall of the University, and in spite of the most heroic efforts on the part of the faculty, students, and town authorities the flames could not be extinguished till they had destroyed the hall, the interior of the rotunda, and many valuable books in the library. The damage was repaired by the erection of buildings that were strictly in accordance with Jefferson's ideas of architecture and handsomer than the old ones. The fire also consumed a famous painting, "The School of Athens," which was a copy of Raphael's celebrated fresco in the Vatican. This was restored as a fresco, Pope Leo XIII having given special permission for the original to be copied.

War with Spain. — In 1895 Cuba, which was a colony of Spain, rebelled for the purpose of winning her independence. For three years the Spaniards tried to put down the rebellion and treated the Cubans with great cruelty. This caused the United States to sympathize with the oppressed Cubans in their effort to win their independence. At a time when public opinion was running high against the Spaniards for the inhuman manner in which they were carrying on the war, an unexpected event brought on a conflict between the United States and Spain. The *Maine*, a battleship of the United States, which was lying in the harbor at Havana, was blown up on the night of February 14, 1898, the explosion killing two officers and two hundred and fifty-eight of the crew. It could not be proved that the Spaniards were responsible for the disaster. Indeed, its cause has never been found *out, but the* effect of the event was to arouse against Spain a war feeling too strong to be repressed. Accordingly President McKinley sent a war message to Congress, the result of which was that Congress responded by adopting a resolution that Cuba should be free, and authorizing the President to use the army and navy of the United States to compel Spain to give up her government of the island. This led to war between the United States and Spain. It was formally declared on April 25.

Virginia's Patriotism. — When President McKinley called for troops to carry on the war with Spain, Virginia responded with enthusiasm, and raised her quota promptly. Her soldiers were soon under arms, and eager for action. They were not, however, called into battle, as most of the fighting was done on the sea, and resulted in one unbroken series of triumphs for the United States.

General Fitzhugh Lee. — At the breaking out of the war, General Fitzhugh Lee, who was a nephew of General Robert E. Lee and had been himself a distinguished Confederate officer, was United States consul-general at Havana. He received the appointment of major general in the United States army, and rendered patriotic and valuable service under the flag he had fought against in the days of the Civil War. He was later put on the retired list of the United States army with the rank of major general.

Results of the War. — The war ended in the defeat of Spain. She was forced to acknowledge the independence of Cuba, and to cede Porto Rico and the Philippine Islands to the United States. More important, however, to the United States than her military success and the acquisition of territory, was the fact brought out by the war that the hostile feelings that had arrayed the North and South against each other during the stormy days of the Civil War and for many years afterwards had at last passed away and that the people of the two sections were now a united people. Never since the close of the Spanish War have designing politicians been able to array the people of the two sections against each other by appealing to the passions that separated them during the Civil War.

QUESTIONS

1. Describe the Capitol disaster.
2. What did General Lee believe to be the duty of all who wished to take part in the restoration of their state?
3. What position did he accept at the close of the Civil War?
4. When did he die, and what is said of him?
5. Was education encouraged in colonial days?
6. What did Governor Berkeley say in regard to free schools?
7. Give a brief account of the present public school system.
8. Give the history of the " White House of the Confederacy."
9. Name the patriotic societies that are sustained by Virginia women.
10. What is said of the patriotism of Virginia women?
11. What was the Yorktown Centennial, and when was it held?
12. Why did Virginia borrow money between 1784 and 1861?
13. What portion of the debt was set apart for West Virginia to pay?
14. Why was any of the debt assigned to West Virginia?
15. Tell what caused the formation of the Readjuster party.
16. Were the Readjusters satisfied with the McCulloch law ?
17. When the Readjusters came into power, what law did they pass, and what did the law provide in regard to the state debt?
18. What caused the Readjuster party to go out of power?
19. When was a settlement finally made with the bondholders?
20. Tell of the debt controversy between Virginia and West Virginia.
21. Describe Virginia's exhibit at the Columbian Exposition.
22. What damage did the fire in 1895 do to the University of Virginia?
23. What caused the war with Spain, and when did it begin?
24. What is said about Virginia's patriotism?
25. What service did General Fitzhugh Lee render to the United States at this time?
26. *What were the results of the war with Spain?*

CHAPTER XXXI

The Constitutional Convention of 1901. — The government of Virginia was carried on for more than thirty years under the constitution framed during the Reconstruction period. This constitution had never been acceptable to the state, as it had not been made by her representative leaders. As the nineteenth century drew to an end, the people became interested in getting a new constitution, one better suited to their needs. In 1901 a convention was called and charged with the duty of making the new constitution. The work was well done. When the new constitution was ready, it was not submitted to the people for approval by vote, but was proclaimed as the fundamental law of the state and promptly accepted as such by all the departments of the state government. It went into operation in 1902.

Important Changes. — Among the changes made by the new constitution, the following are worthy of special mention :

1. A corporation commission was created, with power to supervise corporations and transportation companies, and to grant charters under general laws passed by the legislature.

2. The method of electing the superintendent of public instruction was changed, so that this officer is now elected by the people instead of by the legislature.

3. Provision was made for electing all the members of the state senate every four years, instead of half of them every two years, as was formerly the case.

4. The right to vote was restricted to persons who conform to certain educational qualifications and pay their poll taxes.

5. The county court, which had been an honored institution from the earliest times, was abolished.[1]

Campaign for Better Schools. — By the end of the nineteenth century, the opposition that had existed to the public school system had passed away. The state had grown prosperous and her finances were in good condition. The time seemed ripe for arousing increased interest in public education. In 1902, Dr. Robert Frazer and Harry St. George Tucker were engaged by the Southern Education Board to make addresses to the people of the state upon the importance of improving the schools. They carried on this work energetically and with much success for a year and a half. R. C. Stearnes, then president of the State Teachers' Association, and the teachers generally took an active part in this educational campaign and in forming plans for better school work.

Educational Conference. — Following this preparatory work, in March, 1904, Governor A. J. Montague and Dr. Joseph W. Southall, then superintendent of public instruction, issued a call for a conference in the interest of education. This met in the state senate chamber and was well attended by representative men and women. All present were deeply interested in forming plans "whereby

---

[1] The giving up of the old county court days caused much regret to a large number of citizens, for on these days, which came once a month, it had long been the custom of the people of all classes to gather at the courthouse for *the transaction of* business both public and private, and to discuss politics.

the state should have more practical schools and the interest of the people at large aroused to give coöperative work and support to the improvement of school and community interests." After two days spent in earnest discussion, the Conference [1] organized itself into a permanent body, and has since held annual meetings.

Educational Revival. — The work that had been done brought on a remarkable educational revival, which awakened all through the state an increased interest in the public school system, as the common center of all educational forces. As a result, the funds for school purposes have been greatly increased by both state and local taxation, pupils have attended the schools in larger numbers, many excellent school buildings have been erected, and an appreciation of the value of agriculture and manual training has been aroused.

The Coöperative Education Association. [2] — The interest in better schools awakened by the educational revival is kept alive by the Coöperative Education Association, which was organized at the Conference held in March, 1904. This association has since its formation taken a conspicuous part in interesting the people in the public schools and inducing them to provide better and more sanitary school-

[1] The Conference adopted the following program of purposes:

(1) A nine months' school for every child.

(2) A high school within reasonable distance of every child.

(3) Well-trained teachers for all public schools.

(4) Efficient supervision of schools.

(5) The introduction of agricultural and industrial training into the schools.

(6) The promotion of libraries and correlation of public libraries and public schools.

(7) Schools for the defective and dependent classes.

(8) The organization of a citizens' education association in every county and city.

[2] This was first called the Coöperative Education Commission.

houses, more attractive grounds, and higher salaries for teachers. Indeed, its good influence is actively felt in every movement for the betterment of the schools. The work of the association is greatly forwarded by Citizens' Leagues that have been organized all over the state. These leagues discuss in their meetings plans for school improvement and measures for the betterment of community life.

Leaders in the Educational Revival. — The first president of the Coöperative Education Association was Dr. S. C. Mitchell, under whose leadership it was formed. He was succeeded by J. Stewart Bryan, and he in turn by Mrs. B. B. Munford, its present (1915) efficient head. Mrs. L. R. Dashiell, who was the first person in Virginia to organize citizens' leagues in country neighborhoods, for a number of years did most valuable work as Director of Leagues. J. H. Binford was for five years actively engaged, as executive secretary, in forwarding the aims of the Association. J. D. Eggleston, who in 1905 succeeded Dr. Southall as superintendent of public instruction, proved a most efficient leader in directing the forces of the educational revival. He was followed by R. C. Stearnes, who came into office in 1912, and is now (1915) zealously engaged in carrying on the good work already begun. Many other citizens and teachers could be mentioned as having been actively engaged in bringing on the educational revival.

The Training of Teachers. — For the special training of teachers, the state has made ample provision for men in the normal department of William and Mary College, and for women at normal schools of high grade at Farmville, Fredericksburg, Harrisonburg, and Radford. Excellent facilities for the education of colored teachers have been provided at the Virginia Normal and Industrial Institute *and at the* Hampton Normal and Industrial Institute.

Higher Education. — Virginia is well supplied with institutions for higher education. Some of these belong to the state, while others are sustained by private and church endowment. These institutions give students unsurpassed advantages for obtaining higher and professional education.

Pensions for Teachers. — The legislature, recognizing that the state did not pay her public school teachers salaries sufficiently large for them to accumulate enough for their support in old age, established in 1908 an old age pension system. Part of the fund needed is contributed by the teachers of the public schools, who pay one per cent of their salaries, and the amount thus raised is supplemented by an annual appropriation from the state.

The Jamestown Exposition. — As Virginia was the cradle of the English race in America, it was fitting that she should celebrate in appropriate manner the three hundredth anniversary of the settlement at Jamestown. This she did in 1907 by an exposition which was held on · Hampton Roads, opposite Old Point. It was formally opened by President Roosevelt on April 26 in the presence of many distinguished people. The opening was attended by striking military and naval displays. The array of American and foreign warships was the most imposing ever seen in American waters. The exposition was largely attended and had the happy effect of making the products and resources of the state widely known.

In 1907, also, the old church at Jamestown, with the exception of the tower, was rebuilt as a memorial chapel (page 89).[1]

---

[1] Jamestown Island is now protected from the encroachments of the water by a sea wall built around it by the United States government. On the island, a handsome monument, one hundred feet high, has been erected by the government to commemorate the founding of the nation.

Near it a handsome statue of John Smith has been erected.

The State Health Department. — The State Health Department is rendering most valuable service in teaching the people how to prevent disease. Pamphlets giving information upon this subject have been widely distributed, and lectures have been delivered by Dr. Ennion G. Williams, Commissioner of Health, and other eminent physicians at many points in the state. As a result of this active campaign, the public health is year by year growing better. The outbreaks of typhoid fever are becoming less frequent, and the ravages of consumption are being held in check. The health department, with the aid received from the Rockefeller Sanitary Commission, is waging a successful warfare against the hookworm disease. Thousands of children who had the disease and whose prospects in life had been blighted by it, have been restored to health by proper treatment. The legislature makes an annual appropriation to the health department and its work is supplemented by city and county boards of health.

Need of Good Roads. — The roads in the state were for many years very bad. The native Virginians, accustomed to them from childhood, have always known how to make them serve their purposes of travel, but strangers have found them well-nigh impassable.

The Virginia roads proved a serious obstacle to the British in their invasions of the state during the Revolutionary War, and nearly a hundred years later the same roads added their part in bringing disaster to the Federal armies in many campaigns of the Civil War. Such roads, while serving a good purpose in bringing about the defeat of an *enemy in time of war*, prove a serious drawback to a great state in "piping days of peace," when roads that will forward transportation and not hinder it are needed.

Movement for Good Roads. — The people have in recent years become thoroughly aroused to the importance of having good roads and have come to regard this as a problem of vital importance to all the inhabitants, especially to the residents of the country. The State Highway Commission, created in 1906, and the Rural Road Improvement League, formed in 1914, are rendering valuable service in giving information as to the best method of road building and in arousing public interest.

The movement for good roads is widespread, and, as a consequence of it, the roads are being steadily improved all over the state and their further betterment widely discussed. This movement has been going on for some time, and as a result of it there are already splendid highways running from the mountains to the sea, which add much to the pleasures of life and to the advancement of progress.

Scientific Farming. — The people are becoming much interested in scientific farming. Many influences are help-- ing to bring about this important result. Agricultural high schools have been established by law in the congressional districts — one in each district. These schools are under the direct control of the State Board of Education and are intended to be centers of information in regard to improved methods for their respective districts. Each one must have at least five acres of land for experimental purposes. The boys' corn clubs and the girls' canning clubs are arousing much interest among the young people. These clubs are under the control of the Virginia Polytechnic Institute. Farm demonstrators and special trains full of exhibits, accompanied by lecturers, add their part to the agricultural awakening. Land is increasing in value, and there is a bright outlook for country life. As for its inconveniences, they are materially lessened by the telephone, rural mail delivery, parcel post, and automobiles.

Virginia Fruits. — As a fruit-growing state, Virginia takes high rank. Excellent fruits in great variety are raised, but apples are most extensively cultivated and constitute the most profitable fruit crop of the state. Many of the apples are of fine flavor. Especially is this true of the Albemarle pippin. A barrel of these luscious apples was presented to Queen Victoria by Andrew Stevenson of Albemarle County, who was, some twenty years before the Civil War, United States minister to Great Britain. The pippin at once became the favorite apple of the royal household, and, it is said, has remained so to the present day.

Growth of Towns and Cities. — The towns and cities are growing by leaps and bounds, and a number of them are becoming important commercial centers. Danville has established flourishing cotton mills, and is the largest market in the world for bright, loose tobacco. Lynchburg excels all other cities in the state in the manufacture of shoes, and Roanoke is noted for its machine shops. All through the prosperous Valley of Virginia a steady and healthy growth is going on in the old towns and cities, while new ones are springing up. Lexington and Staunton are known as important educational centers. Newport News, with one of the largest, deepest, and safest harbors on the Atlantic coast, has become a shipbuilding center. Norfolk is the central port on the Atlantic coast for exporting Southern and Western products, and is connected by steamship lines with ports in the United States and foreign countries. Petersburg is noted for its large trunk and bag factory and is a prominent peanut market. Richmond, the *capital city*, has become prominent as a manufacturing city, having many important plants. In 1888 she put in operation the first electric street car line in the United States. She is a reserve city[1] and has one of the United States regional banks,[2] which makes her the banking center of a large section of country. She is to-day making progress with tremendous strides, but remains true to her traditions, and, while taking on the thrift of the present, preserves in a charming manner the culture of the past.

Resources. — The resources of the state, if developed, would produce wealth enough to enrich an empire. The Alleghany region abounds in gold, silver, copper, granite, marble, and coal. Iron ore is found in at least half the counties, and zinc, lead, and tin exist in quantities that indicate profitable investment for capital. These are but a few of the state's mineral resources, which appear to be almost boundless. The climate and soil present conditions favorable to the production of nearly all the useful and profitable agricultural crops of the world. Matthew Fontaine Maury, Virginia's great scientist, who was well acquainted with her resources, said: " The more I search the old state, the more she reminds me of the magic sheaf of wheat, which the more it was threshed the more it yielded ; for the longer I study her valleys and mountains, her waters, climate, and soils, the more I am astonished and impressed at the variety, abundance, and value of her un-

[1] For financial purposes, the United States is divided into twelve districts, in each of which a city is selected as the center of the district's financial operations. This is called a Federal Reserve city. Richmond is the Federal Reserve city for the fifth district, which consists of the District of Columbia, Maryland, Virginia, North Carolina, South Carolina, and all West Virginia except the panhandle counties.

[2] All the national banks in a district join and form a bank, in which each takes stock to the amount of six per cent of its own capital and surplus. The bank thus formed by the national banks is called a regional bank.

developed treasure. And the vastness of the wealth which lies dormant in her borders, waiting for capital and labor to develop and utilize it, fairly dazzles the imagination."

Progress. — The people are still mainly engaged in agriculture, but at the same time they realize that this is not the only source of wealth and advancement, and so they are paying attention to other branches of industry. Manufactures are being established, factories are springing up, blast furnaces are being reared, and mines developed. Cattle raising is very profitable, and the newly developed business of truck farming is giving most encouraging results. Virginia wheat is of such excellent quality that flour made from it is in great demand outside of the state, which renders the milling interest a flourishing one. Small industries, such as the making of staves, tubs, etc., are steadily increasing. The shipment of furniture and ornamental woods is rendering the products of the forest valuable. All these and many other industrial enterprises that are being developed mark a new era of progress for the Old Dominion.

State-wide Prohibition. — In 1914 there was a hotly contested campaign for state-wide prohibition. The advocates of both sides strongly represented their cause in public meetings and flooded the state with literature. The people became thoroughly aroused on the question, and a full vote was polled. The result was a majority of about thirty thousand in favor of state-wide prohibition. The legislature, at its next regular session, will enact the will of the people into a law, and in 1916 Virginia will take her place among the prohibition states.

The prohibition forces were ably led to victory by Dr. James Cannon, Jr.

Lack of Early Literature. — American literature had its *beginning in* accounts of travel and adventure written by

Captain John Smith and other early settlers. But during colonial days, and indeed up to the time of the Civil War, the conditions of life in Virginia were not favorable to the development of literary activity. The plantation system, which rendered personal effort unnecessary, encouraged the educated classes to lead lives of leisure and to regard literature as an accomplishment rather than as a serious calling. There was, too, a lack of towns and cities to furnish centers of literary life, and without these writing as a profession is never profitable. The ambitious turned to law and politics as offering easier avenues to distinction. " Literature stood no chance, because the ambition of young men of the South was universally turned in the direction of political distinction, and because the monopoly of advancement held by the profession of law was too well established and too clearly recognized to admit of its claim being contested." [1] The eloquent orations of Patrick Henry, the able state papers of Washington, Jefferson, Madison, and Monroe, the writings of Chief Justice Marshall,[2] and other productions that might be cited, prove that the lack of progress in literature was not due to want of intellectual ability.

[1] "The Old South," by Thomas Nelson Page, p. 67.

[2] John Marshall (1755–1835) was born in Virginia. In his early manhood he served for five years in the Revolutionary War, and after this he began the practice of law. In 1797 he was sent as Envoy Extraordinary to France, and in 1800 he became Secretary of State under President Adams. In 1801 he was appointed Chief Justice of the United States, and was for thirty-four years at the head of the Judicial Department of the government. His decisions gave the Supreme Court a reputation which has never been surpassed. The fidelity and remarkable ability with which he discharged the duties of his high office caused it to be said of him that " he was born to be the chief justice of any country in which he lived." Judge Story paid the following tribute to Marshall, " His judgments for power of thought, beauty of illustration, and elegance of demonstration are justly numbered among the highest reaches of human thought."

Development of Literature. — The Civil War brought changes in the social, industrial, and educational conditions. Hardly had the state solved the most difficult problems that followed the Civil War before it became apparent that literature had experienced a quickening impulse. One by one Virginia authors obtained a hearing from the public and won distinction. Among these are to be found historians, poets, and novelists. While the time has not come to make a final estimate of the work of these writers, as most of them are still living and increasing in reputation as authors, yet it may be said that they will compare favorably with those of any other English-speaking country. The indications are that, as a result of this new movement in literature, the Virginia of the past will be seen again in memory's soft light, and the Virginia of the future will not lack for literary representatives.

Influence of Virginia on the Nation. — The influence of Virginia is still strongly felt on the nation. In 1912 Woodrow Wilson, a Virginian by birth, eminent as an educator, historian, and statesman, was elected president of the United States. The good effects of his progressive policy in regard to the tariff, the currency, and other great questions will long be felt upon our national life. In dealing with foreign nations, he has by his tact and judgment preserved peace at times when war seemed almost unavoidable. Not only in the high office of the presidency, but also in other departments of the national government, Virginians are wielding an influence so great that the Old Dominion is still entitled to the name " Mother of Statesmen " given her in the early days of the Republic.

Virginia Honors her Great Men. — Virginia does not forget her distinguished men, as is shown by the large *number of* monuments that have been erected in the state.

In the Capitol Square at Richmond there is an equestrian statue of Washington, and upon its pedestal are grouped statues of the leaders of the Revolutionary period — Mason holding the Bill of Rights, Jefferson with the Declaration of Independence, Thomas Nelson as the represent-

Birthplace of Woodrow Wilson at Staunton, Va.

ative of finance, John Marshall, the great jurist, with a book of law, Patrick Henry with his sword drawn, and Andrew Lewis, rifle in hand. A little distance from this group there is a statue of Stonewall Jackson, which was presented to the state by his English admirers; and, in other parts of the city, an equestrian statue of Lee, a statue of A. P. Hill, also one in honor of the soldiers and sailors of the Confederacy. A monument to Stuart stands near Yellow Tavern, where he fell, and a statue of him has been erected in Richmond. A monument in Hollywood to President John Tyler has been erected by the United States government. In many other parts of the state, especially at the courthouses, memorials have been erected to the Old Dominion's noble dead.[1] The old soldiers

The Jackson Statue at Richmond

who are in need the state pensions as liberally as her revenue will permit. **Tablet in Memory of Pocahontas.** — Within the walls of the Memorial Chapel on Jamestown Island a handsome tablet in memory of Pocahontas was unveiled October 24, 1914. The presentation address was made by Dr. Lyon G. Tyler, president of William and Mary College, who recounted in eloquent words the deeds of daring and sacrifice, which the tablet commemorated, done by the Indian princess in befriending the early English settlers. The tablet was the gift of the Washington branch of the Association for the Preservation of Virginia Antiquities. It was fittingly placed in the walls of the Memorial Chapel next to a tablet in honor of John Smith.

[1] A statue of Dr. Hunter McGuire, Stonewall Jackson's chief medical director, stands in the Capitol Square, and near by one of Governor William Smith. In Monroe Park there are statues of General W. C. Wickham, a noted Confederate officer, and Joseph Bryan, one of Richmond's most progressive and philanthropic citizens. In Lynchburg a statue has been erected of John W. Daniel, who was for twenty-three years an able representative of *Virginia in the* United States Senate.

The Present Governor.[1] — In 1913 Henry Carter Stuart of Russell County was nominated for governor without opposition and elected almost unanimously — a double compliment never before paid a candidate for the chief executive office. His induction into office was marked by a great military parade, and the inaugural address was delivered from the portico of the Capitol. Since the new administration began, the governor's mansion has been the scene of many brilliant social functions which have been much enjoyed by the members of the legislature, the citizens of Richmond, and the people of the state at large. In his official capacity Governor Stuart has shown himself to be in full sympathy with all progressive movements for the good of the people. He bears a name that all Virginians delight to honor; for he is a nephew of that distinguished Confederate general, J. E. B. Stuart.

Conclusion. — Since Virginia resumed her place in the sisterhood of states, she has been steadily increasing in prosperity. In character the people are unchanged. They continue to display the same devotion to duty and principle that has ever characterized them, and they cherish their rights as strongly as they did in former years. Whatever changes may come, it is safe to predict, in the light of the past, that when the future history of the free, noble, high-minded people of the Old Dominion is written, it will contain a record of deeds that will be worthy of the countrymen of Washington and Lee.

[1] The governors elected since the Civil War have been Gilbert C. Walker, James L. Kemper, F. W. M. Holliday, William E. Cameron, Fitzhugh Lee, Philip W. McKinney, Charles T. O'Ferrall, J. Hoge Tyler, Andrew J. Montague, Claude A. Swanson, William Hodges Mann, Henry Carter Stuart.

QUESTIONS

1. Why was Virginia not satisfied with her constitution, and when did she call a convention to make a new one?
2. Mention some of the important changes brought about by the new constitution.
3. Why was a campaign for better schools started in 1902?
4. Tell about the formation of the Education Conference, and state briefly its objects.
5. What was the effect of the educational revival?
6. Tell about the work of the Coöperative Education Association.
7. Mention some of the leaders of the educational revival.
8. What does Virginia do for the training of her teachers?
9. What is said about Virginia's institutions for higher education?
10. What has been done in regard to pensions for public school teachers?
11. When was the Jamestown Exposition held, and what did it do for the state?
12. What valuable work is the State Health Department doing?
13. What is said about the bad roads of Virginia, and what improvements are now being made?
14. What has caused an interest in scientific farming?
15. How does Virginia stand as a fruit-growing state, and what is her most profitable fruit crop?
16. What is said of the growth of towns and cities in Virginia?
17. For what are some of the towns and cities most noted?
18. Mention some of the resources of Virginia.
19. What does Matthew Fontaine Maury say of the state?
20. What are some of the branches of industry that indicate the progress of the state?
21. What was the result of the election on the question of state-wide prohibition?
22. Why was there a lack of early literature?
23. How did plantation life retard its growth?
24. To what professions did the young men turn, and why?
25. What proves that there was not a lack of intellectual ability?
26. What is said of the development of literature after the Civil War?
27. Give reasons why the influence of Virginia is still strongly felt on the nation?

28. In what way does Virginia honor her great men ?
29. Mention the names of some to whom monuments have been raised.
30. Give an account of the unveiling of the tablet to Pocahontas.
31. What is said of the administration of Governor Stuart ?
32. What may be safely predicted in regard to the future history of Virginia ?

REVIEW QUESTIONS

1. Give an outline of the condition of Virginia after the Civil War, and of the steps that led to the appointment of a provisional governor.
2. Why was she refused readmission into the Union, and under what rule was she placed by Congress ?
3. Why did the administration of the government fall into the hands of " Carpet-baggers " and " Scalawags" ? Describe their rule.
4. When did Virginia reënter the Union, and what change did this bring in the administration of her government ?
5. What object did the United States have in establishing the Freedmen's Bureau, and what false expectation did it cause among the negroes ?
6. How long had the plantation system existed, and what caused its destruction ?
7. What spirit have the Virginians always shown, and how did it manifest itself during the Reconstruction period ?
8. How did General Lee, by his example, keep many Virginians from leaving the state ? How and where did he spend his last years ?
9. Give a short account of the public school system of Virginia. Who was its first superintendent ?
10. Give a history of the Confederate museum in Richmond. What patriotic societies are sustained by the women of Virginia, and what is said of their patriotism ?
11. Give a brief account of the state debt and of the Readjuster party.
12. What caused the war with Spain to break out ? How did Virginia show her patriotism in this war ?
13. Mention several impórtant changes made by the constitution adopted in 1902.
14. Give an account of the campaign for better schools and its results.
15. What provision has the state made for the special training of her teachers and for giving them pensions ?

16. How have the people of Virginia, in recent times, shown their interest in the betterment of health and in the improvement of roads and farming?
17. Mention some of the resources of the state, and tell about her progress.
18. Explain the reason why literature did not flourish before the Civil War, and give its present outlook.
19. In what way does the Old Dominion specially honor some of her distinguished men?
20. What qualities do Virginians continue to display, and what is predicted of their future?

CHRONOLOGICAL TABLE OF IMPORTANT EVENTS (1860-1914)

1860. Abraham Lincoln elected President.
1861. Southern Confederacy formed at Montgomery, February 8.
1861. Jefferson Davis inaugurated President of the Confederacy, February 18.
1861. Lincoln inaugurated President of the United States, March 4.
1861. Fort Sumter captured by the Confederates, April 14.
1861. Lincoln's call for 75,000 volunteers, April 15.
1861. Secession of Virginia, April 17.
1861. Confederate capital changed from Montgomery to Richmond.
1861. Battle of Big Bethel, June 10.
1861. West Virginia organized a separate government, June 11.
1861. Confederate Congress assembled at Richmond, July 20.
1861. First battle of Manassas, July 21.
1862. Battle between the *Virginia* and the *Monitor*, March 9.
1862. Jackson's Valley Campaign, March-June.
1862. Battle of Seven Pines, May 31-June 1.
1862. General Lee made commander of the Army of Northern Virginia in June.
1862. The Seven Days' battle around Richmond, June 25-July 1.
1862. Second battle of Manassas, August 29-30.
1862. Harper's Ferry captured by Jackson, September 15.
1862. General Lee invaded Maryland in September.
1862. Battle of Sharpsburg, or Antietam, September 17.
1862. Battle of Fredericksburg, December 13.

1863. Emancipation Proclamation, January 1.
1863. Battle of Chancellorsville, May 2-3.
1863. Death of Stonewall Jackson, May 10.
1863. West Virginia admitted into the Union, June 20.
1863. Battle of Gettysburg, July 1-3.
1864. Battles of the Wilderness, May 5-6.
1864. Battle of Spottsylvania Courthouse, May 8-12.
1864. Battle of New Market, May 15.
1864. Battle of Cold Harbor, June 3.
1864. Siege of Petersburg begun, June 15.
1864. Invasion of Maryland and Pennsylvania by Early in July.
1864. Mine explosion at Petersburg and battle of the Crater, July 30.
1865. Richmond evacuated, April 2.
1865. General Lee surrendered, April 9.
1865. Provisional government established in Virginia, May 9.
1865. Assassination of President Lincoln, April 14.
1865. President Davis taken prisoner, May 10.
1865. Slavery abolished in the United States.
1866. Memorial Day instituted.
1867. Reconstruction Acts passed by Congress.
1870. Virginia readmitted into the Union.
1870. The Capitol disaster.
1870. Public school system established.
1870. Death of General Robert E. Lee.
1881. Readjuster party comes into power.
1892. Settlement with the bondholders.
1893. World's Columbian Exposition.
1898. War with Spain.
1902. New constitution adopted.
1907. Jamestown Exposition.
1914. Unveiling of tablet to Pocahontas.

APPENDIX

COLONIAL GOVERNORS

FROM SETTLEMENT OF VIRGINIA TILL REVOLUTION

1.	1607.	Edward Maria Wingfield (Pres.).	25.	1677.	Herbert Jeffries (Lt. Gov.).
2.	1607.	John Ratcliffe (Pres.).	26.	1677.	Herbert Jeffries.
3.	1608.	John Smith (Pres.).	27.	1678.	Henry Chicheley.
4.	1609.	George Percy (Pres.).	28.	1678.	Thomas, Lord Culpeper.
5.	1609.	Thomas West, Lord Delaware.	29.	1680.	Henry Chicheley (Lt. Gov.).
6.	1611.	Thomas Dale (High Marshal).	30.	1684.	Lord Howard of Effingham.
7.	1616.	George Yeardley (Lt. Gov.).	31.	1689.	Nathaniel Bacon (Lt. Gov.).
8.	1617.	Samuel Argall (Lt. Gov.).	32.	1690.	Francis Nicholson.
9.	1619.	George Yeardley.	33.	1692.	Edmund Andros.
10.	1621.	Francis Wyatt.	34.	1698.	Francis Nicholson.
11.	1626.	George Yeardley.	35.	1704.	Earl of Orkney.
12.	1627.	Francis West.	36.	1705.	Edward Nott (Lt. Gov.).
13.	1628.	John Potts.	37.	1706.	Edmund Jennings (Lt. Gov.).
14.	1629.	John Harvey.			
15.	1635.	John West.	38.	1710.	Robert Hunter (Lt. Gov.).
16.	1635.	John Harvey.	39.	1710.	Alexander Spotswood (Lt. Gov.).
17.	1639.	Francis Wyatt.			
18.	1641.	William Berkeley.	40.	1722.	Hugh Drysdale (Lt. Gov.).
19.	1645.	Richard Kemp (Lt. Gov.).			
20.	1645.	William Berkeley.	41.	1726.	Robert Carter (Lt. Gov.).
21.	1652.	Richard Bennet.			
22.	1656.	Edward Diggs.	42.	1727.	William Gooch (Lt. Gov.).
23.	1658.	Samuel Matthews			
24.	1660.	William Berkeley.			

276

43. 1749. John Robinson, Sr. (Lt. Gov.).
44. 1749. Lord Albemarle.
45. 1750. Louis Burwell (Lt. Gov.).
46. 1752. Robert Dinwiddie (Lt. Gov.).
47. 1758. John Blair (Lt. Gov.).
48. 1758. Francis Fauquier.
49. 1768. John Blair (Lt. Gov.).
50. 1768. Norborne Berkeley de Botetourt.
51. 1770. William Nelson (Lt. Gov.).
52. 1772. John, Lord Dunmore.

GOVERNORS OF VIRGINIA FROM 1776

1. **Patrick Henry**, elected 1776, Patriot or Whig. Born, Hanover County, April 2, 1736. Died, Charlotte County, June 6, 1799, aged 63.

2. **Thomas Jefferson**, elected 1779, Patriot or Whig. Born, Albemarle County, April 2, 1743. Died July 4, 1826. Aged 83.

3. **Thomas Nelson**, elected 1781, Patriot or Whig. Born, Yorktown, December 26, 1738. Died, Hanover County, January 4, 1789, aged 51.

4. **Benjamin Harrison**, elected 1781, Patriot or Whig. Born at Charles City County, ——, 1740. Died, Charles City County, ——, 1791, aged 51.

5. **Patrick Henry**, elected 1784, Patriot or Whig. Born, Hanover County, April 2, 1736. Died, Charlotte County, June 6, 1799, aged 63.

6. **Edmund Randolph**, elected 1786, Patriot or Whig. Born, Williamsburg, August 10, 1753. Died, Clarke County, September 13, 1813, aged 60.

7. **Beverly Randolph**, elected 1788, Patriot or Whig. Born, Henrico County, ——, 1754. Died, Cumberland County, ——, 1797, aged 43.

8. **Henry Lee**, elected 1791, Republican. Born, Westmoreland County, January 29, 1756. Died, Cumberland Island, Ga., March 25, 1818, aged 62.

9. **Robert Brooke**, elected 1794, Republican. Born, Spottsylvania County, ——, 1761. Died, Richmond, ——, 1799, aged 38.

10. **James Wood**, elected 1796, Republican. Born, Frederick County, ——, 1750. Died, Richmond, July 16, 1813, aged 63.

11. **James Monroe**, elected 1799, Republican. Born, Westmoreland County, April 28, 1758. Died, New York, N. Y., July 4, 1831, aged 73.

12. **John Page**, elected 1802, Republican. Born, Gloucester County, April 17, 1744. Died, Richmond, October 11, 1808, aged 64.

13. **William H. Cabell**, elected 1805, Republican. Born, Cumberland County, December 16, 1772. Died, Richmond, June 17, 1853, aged 81.

14. **John Tyler**, elected 1808, Republican. Born, Williamsburg, ——, 1748. Died, Charles City County, January 6, 1813, aged 65.

15. **James Monroe**, elected 1811. Born, Westmoreland County, April 28, 1758. Died, New York City, July 4, 1831, aged 73.

16. **George W. Smith**, elected 1811, Republican. Born, Essex County, ——, 1762. Died, Richmond, December 26, 1811, aged 49.

17. **James Barbour**, elected 1812, Republican. Born, Orange County, June 10, 1775. Died, Orange County, June 8, 1842, aged 67.

18. **Wilson C. Nicholas**, elected 1814, Republican. Born, Hanover County, ——, 1757. Died, Milton, October 10, 1820, aged 63.

19. **James P. Preston**, elected 1816, Republican. Born, Montgomery County, ——, 1774. Died, Isle of Wight County, May 4, 1843, aged 69.

20. **Thomas M. Randolph**, elected 1819, Republican. Born, Tuckahoe, October 1, 1768. Died, Charlottesville, June 20, 1828, aged 60.

21. **James Pleasants**, elected 1822, Republican. Born, Goochland County, October 24, 1769. Died, Goochland County, November 9, 1839, aged 70.

22. **John Tyler**, elected 1825, Republican. Born, Charles City County, March 29, 1790. Died, Richmond, January 18, 1862, aged 72.

23. **William B. Giles**, elected 1827, State-Rights Democrat. Born, Amelia County, August 12, 1762. Died, Albemarle County, December 4, 1830, aged 68.

24. **John Floyd**, elected 1830, State-Rights Democrat. Born, Jefferson County, Ky., April 24, 1783. Died, Sweet Springs, August 16, 1837, aged 54.

25. **L. W. Tazewell**, elected 1834, State-Rights Whig. Born, Williamsburg, December 17, 1774. Died, Norfolk, March 6, 1860, aged 86.

26. **Wyndham Robertson**, elected 1836, State-Rights Whig. Born, Manchester, January 26, 1803. Died, Washington County, February 11, 1888, aged 85.

27. **David Campbell**, elected 1837, Democrat. Born, Washington County, August 2, 1779. Died, Abingdon, March 19, 1859, aged 80.

28. **Thomas W. Gilmer**, elected 1840, State-Rights Whig. Born, Albemarle County, April 6, 1802. Died, Richmond, February 28, 1844, aged 42.

29. **John M. Patton**, elected 1841, State-Rights Whig. Born, Fredericksburg, August 10, 1797. Died, Richmond, October 28, 1858, aged 61.

30. **John Rutherford**, elected 1841, State-Rights Democrat. Born, Richmond city, December 6, 1792. Died, Richmond, July —, 1866, aged 74.

31. **John M. Gregory**, elected 1842, State-Rights Whig. Born, Charles City County, July 8, 1804. Died, Richmond, April 9, 1884, aged 80.

32. **James McDowell**, elected 1843, Democrat. Born, Rockbridge County, October 12, 1796. Died, Rockbridge County, August 24, 1851, aged 55.

33. **William Smith**, elected 1846, State-Rights Democrat. Born, King George County, September 6, 1796. Died, Warrenton, May 18, 1887, aged 91.

34. **John B. Floyd**, elected 1849, State-Rights Democrat. Born, Blacksburg, June 1, 1807. Died, Abingdon, August 26, 1863, aged 56.

35. **Joseph Johnson**, elected 1852, State-Rights Democrat. Born, Orange County, N. Y., December 19, 1785. Died, Bridgeport, W. Va., February 27, 1877, aged 92.

36. **Henry A. Wise**, elected 1856, State-Rights Democrat. Born, Accomac County, December 3, 1806. Died, Richmond, September 12, 1876, aged 70.

37. **John Letcher**, elected 1860, State-Rights Democrat. Born, Lexington, March 29, 1813. Died, Lexington, January 26, 1884, aged 71.

38. **William Smith**, elected 1864, State-Rights Democrat. Born, King George County, September 6, 1796. Died, Warrenton, May 18, 1887, aged 91.

39. **Francis H. Pierpont**, appointed 1865, Republican. Born, Monongalia County, West Va., January 25, 1814. Died, ——, 1899.

40. **Henry H. Wells**, appointed 1868, Republican. Born, Rochester, N.Y., September 17, 1823.

41. **Gilbert C. Walker**, elected 1869, Republican. Born, Binghamton, N. Y., August 1, 1832. Died, Binghamton, N. Y., May 11, 1885, aged 53.

42. **James L. Kemper**, elected 1873, Conservative. Born, Madison County, June 11, 1823. Died, Orange County, April 7, 1895.

43. **F. W. M. Holliday**, elected 1877, Conservative. Born, Winchester, February 22, 1828. Died, Winchester, ——, 1899.

44. **William E. Cameron**, elected 1881, Readjuster. Born, Petersburg, November 29, 1842.

45. **Fitzhugh Lee**, elected 1885, Democrat. Born, Fairfax County, November 19, 1835. Died April 28, 1905.

46. **Philip W. McKinney**, elected 1889, Democrat. Born, Buckingham County, March 17, 1832. Died, Farmville, ——, 1899.

47. **Charles T. O'Ferrall**, elected 1893, Democrat. Born, Frederick County, Va., October 21, 1840.

48. **J. Hoge Tyler**, elected 1897, Democrat. Born, Caroline County, Va., August 11, 1846.

49. **Andrew J. Montague**, elected 1901, Democrat. Born, Campbell County, Va., October 3. 1862.

50. **Claude A. Swanson**, elected 1905, Democrat. Born, Pittsylvania County, Va., March 31, 1862.

51. **William Hodges Mann**, elected 1909, Democrat. Born, Williamsburg, July 30, 1843.

52. **Henry Carter Stuart**, elected 1913, Democrat. Born, Wytheville, January 18, 1855.

THE VIRGINIA RESOLVES, 1769

RESOLVES OF THE HOUSE OF BURGESSES, PASSED THE 16TH OF MAY, 1769

Resolved, *Nemine* } That the sole right of imposing taxes on the *Contradicente*, } inhabitants of this His Majesty's Colony and Dominion of Virginia is now, and ever hath been, legally and constitutionally vested in the House of Burgesses, lawfully convened, according to the ancient and established practice, with the consent of the Council, and of His Majesty the King of Great Britain, or his Governor for the time being.

Resolved, *nemine contradicente*, That it is the undoubted privilege of the inhabitants of this colony to petition their Sovereign for redress of grievances; and that it is lawful and expedient to procure the concurrence of His Majesty's other colonies, in dutiful addresses, praying the royal interposition in favor of the violated rights of America.

Resolved, *nemine contradicente*, That all trials for treason, misprision of treason, or for any felony or crime whatsoever, committed and done in this His Majesty's said colony and dominion, by any person or persons residing therein, ought of right to be had, and conducted in and before His Majesty's courts, held within his said colony, according to the fixed and known course of proceeding; and that the seizing any person or persons residing in the colony, suspected of any crime whatsoever, committed therein, and sending such person or persons to places beyond the sea to be tried, is highly derogatory of the rights of British subjects, as thereby the inestimable privilege of being tried by a jury from the vicinage, as well as the liberty of summoning and producing witnesses on such trial, will be taken away from the party accused.

Resolved, *nemine contradicente*, That an humble, dutiful and loyal address be presented to His Majesty, to assure him of our inviolable attachment to his sacred person and government; and to beseech his royal interposition, as the father of all his people, however remote from the seat of his empire, to quiet the minds of his loyal subjects of this colony, and to avert from them those dangers and miseries which will ensue, from the seizing and carrying beyond sea any person residing in America, suspected of any crime whatsoever, to be tried in any other manner than by the ancient and long-established course of proceeding.

(The following order is likewise in their journal of that date) :

Ordered, That the speaker of this House do transmit, without delay, to the speakers of the several houses of Assembly on this continent, a copy of the resolutions now agreed to by this House, requesting their concurrence therein.

ORDINANCE OF SECESSION

AN ORDINANCE TO REPEAL THE RATIFICATION OF THE CONSTITUTION OF THE UNITED STATES OF AMERICA BY THE STATE OF VIRGINIA, AND TO RESUME ALL THE RIGHTS AND POWERS GRANTED UNDER SAID CONSTITUTION

The people of Virginia, in their ratification of the Constitution of the United States of America, adopted by them in convention on the 25th day of June, in the year of our Lord 1788, having declared that the powers granted under said Constitution were derived from the people of the *United States,* and might be resumed whensoever the same should be perverted to their injury and oppression, and the *Federal Government* having perverted said powers, not only to the injury of the *people of Virginia,* but to the oppression of the *Southern slaveholding States:*

Now, therefore, we, the *people of Virginia, do declare and ordain,* That the ordinance adopted by the people of this State in convention on the 25th of June, in the year of our Lord 1788, whereby the Constitution of the United States of America was ratified, and all acts of the General Assembly of this State ratifying or adopting amendments to said Constitution, are hereby *repealed* and *abrogated;* that the union between the State of Virginia and the other States under the Constitution aforesaid is hereby dissolved, and that the State of Virginia is in the full possession and exercise of all the rights of sovereignty which belong and appertain to *a free and independent State.*

And they do further declare, That the said Constitution of the United States of America is no longer binding on any of the citizens of this State.

This ordinance shall take effect and be an act of this day, when ratified by a majority of the votes of the people of this State cast at a poll to be taken thereon on the fourth Thursday in May next, in pursuance of a schedule hereafter to be enacted.

Done in Convention, in the city of Richmond, on the 17th day of April, in the year of our Lord 1861, and in the eighty-fifth year of the *Commonwealth* of Virginia.

PREAMBLE AND BILL OF RIGHTS

(From the State Constitution.)

Whereas, pursuant to an act of the General Assembly of Virginia, approved March the fifth, in the year of our Lord nineteen hundred, the question, "shall there be a convention to revise the Constitution and amend the same?" was submitted to the electors of the State of Virginia, qualified to vote for members of the General Assembly, at an election held throughout the State on the fourth Thursday in May, in the year nineteen hundred, at which election a majority of the electors so qualified voting at said election did decide in favor of a convention for such purpose; and,

Whereas, the General Assembly at its next session did provide by law for the election of delegates to such convention, in pursuance whereof the members of this Convention were elected by the good people of Virginia, to meet in convention for such purpose.

We, therefore, the people of Virginia, so assembled in Convention through our representatives, with gratitude to God for His past favors, and invoking His blessings upon the result of our deliberations, do ordain and establish the following revised and amended Constitution for the government of the Commonwealth:

ARTICLE I.

BILL OF RIGHTS.

A DECLARATION OF RIGHTS, made by the representatives of the good people of Virginia assembled in full and free Convention; which rights do pertain to them and their posterity, as the Basis and Foundation of Government.

SECTION 1. That all men are by nature equally free and independent, and have certain inherent rights, of which, when they enter into a state of society, they cannot, by any compact, deprive or divest their posterity; namely, the enjoyment of life and liberty, with the means of acquiring and possessing property, and pursuing and obtaining happiness and safety.

SEC. 2. That all power is vested in, and consequently derived from, the people; that magistrates are their trustees and servants, and at all times amenable to them.

SEC. 3. That government is, or ought to be, instituted for the common benefit, protection and security of the people, nation or community; of all the various modes and forms of government, that is best, which is capable of producing the greatest degree of happiness and safety, and is most effectually secured against the danger of maladministration; and, whenever any government shall be found inadequate or contrary to these purposes, a majority of the community hath an indubitable, inalienable, and indefeasible right to reform, alter or abolish it, in such manner as shall be judged most conducive to the public weal.

SEC. 4. That no man, or set of men, is entitled to exclusive or separate emoluments or privileges from the community, but in consideration of public services; which not being descendible, neither ought the offices of magistrate, legislator or judge to be hereditary.

SEC. 5. That the legislative, executive, and judicial departments of the State should be separate and distinct; and that the members thereof may be restrained from oppression, by feeling and participating the burthens of the people, they should, at fixed periods, be reduced to a private station, return into that body from which they were originally taken, and the vacancies be supplied by regular elections, in which all or any part of the former members shall be again eligible, or ineligible, as the laws may direct.

SEC. 6. That all elections ought to be free; and that all men, having sufficient evidence of permanent common interest with, and attachment to, the community, have the right of suffrage, and cannot be taxed, or deprived of, or damaged in, their property for public uses, without their own consent, or that of their representatives duly elected, or bound by any law to which they have not, in like manner, assented for the public good.

SEC. 7. That all power of suspending laws, or the execution of laws, by any authority, without consent of the representatives of the people, is injurious to their rights, and ought not to be exercised.

SEC. 8. That no man shall be deprived of his life, or liberty, except by the law of the land, or the judgment of his peers; nor shall any man be compelled in any criminal proceeding to give evidence against himself, nor be put twice in jeopardy for the same offence, but an appeal may be allowed to the Commonwealth in all prosecutions for the violation of a law relating to the state revenue.

That in all criminal prosecutions a man hath a right to demand the cause and nature of his accusation, to be confronted with the accusers and witnesses, to call for evidence in his favor, and to a speedy trial by an impartial jury of his vicinage, without whose unanimous consent he cannot be found guilty; provided, however, that in any criminal case, upon a plea of guilty, tendered in person by the accused, and with the consent of the attorney for the Commonwealth, entered of record, the court shall, and in a prosecution for an offence not punishable by death, or confinement in the penitentiary, upon a plea of not guilty, with the consent of the accused, given in person, and of the attorney for the Commonwealth, both entered of record, the court, in its discretion, may hear and determine the case, without the intervention of a jury; and, that the General Assembly may provide for the trial of offences not punishable by death, or confinement in the penitentiary, by a justice of the peace, without a jury, preserving in all such cases, the right of the accused to an appeal to and trial by jury in the circuit or corporation court; and may also provide for juries consisting of less than twelve, but not less than five, for the trial of offences not punishable by death, or confinement in the penitentiary, and may classify such cases, and prescribe the number of jurors for each class.

SEC. 9. That excessive bail ought not to be required, nor excessive fines imposed, nor cruel and unusual punishments inflicted.

SEC. 10. That general warrants, whereby an officer or messenger may be commanded to search suspected places without evidence of a fact committed, or to seize any person or persons not named, or whose offence is not particularly described and supported by evidence, are grievous and oppressive, and ought not to be granted.

SEC. II. That no person shall be deprived of his property without due process of law; and in controversies respecting property, and in suits between man and man, trial by jury is preferable to any other, and ought to be held sacred; but the General Assembly may limit the number of jurors for civil cases in circuit and corporation courts to not less than five in cases now cognizable by justices of the peace, or to not less than seven in cases not so cognizable.

SEC. 12. That the freedom of the press is one of the great bulwarks of liberty, and can never be restrained but by despotic governments; and any citizen may freely speak, write and publish his sentiments on all subjects, being responsible for the abuse of that right.

SEC. 13. That a well-regulated militia, composed of the body of the people, trained to arms, is the proper, natural and safe defence of a free state; that standing armies, in time of peace should be avoided as dangerous to liberty; and that in all cases the military should be under strict subordination to, and governed by, the civil power.

SEC. 14. That the people have a right to uniform government; and, therefore, that no government separate from, or independent of, the government of Virginia, ought to be erected or established within the limits thereof.

SEC. 15. That no free government, or the blessing of liberty, can be preserved to any people, but by a firm adherence to justice, moderation, temperance, frugality and virtue, and by frequent recurrence to fundamental principles.

SEC. 16. That religion, or the duty which we owe to our Creator, and the manner of discharging it, can be directed only by reason and conviction, not by force or violence; and, therefore, all men are equally entitled to the free exercise of religion, according to the dictates of conscience; and that it is the mutual duty of all to practice Christian forbearance, love and charity towards each other.

SEC. 17. The rights enumerated in this Bill of Rights shall not be construed to limit other rights of the people not therein expressed.

INDEX

---•o•---

287

CPSIA information can be obtained
at www.ICGtesting.com
Printed in the USA
BVHW04s2201160918
527691BV00008B/41/P